INTERNATIONAL COMMUNICATION AND THE NEW DIPLOMACY

Indiana University International Studies

A publication of the
Edward R. Murrow Center of Public Diplomacy

International Communication and the New Diplomacy

Edited by
Arthur S. Hoffman

Indiana University Press

Bloomington and London

DEDICATION

"Truth . . . and personal integrity." That was the
legacy of Edward R. Murrow.

Ed Murrow understood,
as well as any man in our century,
the responsibility—and the power for good—
of modern mass communication.

Hubert H. Humphrey
*Vice President
of the United States*

CONTENTS

PREFACE

This book stems from the personal generosity of the pioneer American communicator Edward L. Bernays, whose Bernays Foundation sponsored the lecture series out of which this book grew. The lectures were delivered in 1965-66 during the inaugural year of the Edward R. Murrow Center of Public Diplomacy, as its first major effort at public service.

Arthur S. Hoffman
USIA Murrow Fellow,
1965-66

Edward R. Murrow Center of Public Diplomacy
Fletcher School of Law and Diplomacy
Tufts University

INTERNATIONAL
COMMUNICATION
AND THE
NEW DIPLOMACY

I

INTRODUCTION

Robert Finley Delaney
Edward R. Murrow Center of Public Diplomacy

The new diplomacy, or "public diplomacy," has been defined as the ways in which both governments and private individuals and groups influence directly or indirectly those public attitudes and opinions which bear directly on other governments' foreign policy decisions. In a sense, public diplomacy is at least as old as Moses' successful attempts to influence the Pharaoh by pressuring his subjects. Almost as ancient is the debate over the proper relationship between the man of learning and the statesman. But today the diplomatic drama is far more complex than in biblical times: the nation-actors are more numerous, their cultural heritages more varied, their clashes more advertised, their weapons more deadly.

We live in a world beset by the frustrations and dilemmas arising from the interaction of individuals, groups, and nations. In the eighteenth and early nineteenth centuries international relations were mainly between governments, and diplomacy was regulated by a formal code of behavior which defined the ground rules for movements on the chess board of power politics. But the old diplomacy died with the technological innovations that produced our modern network of mass communications. Today, rivalry between princes has given way to a confrontation of nations with nations, individuals with individuals, and ideas with ideas. The revolution of mass communications has in turn given rise to the new "public" diplomacy, whose techniques are as yet imperfectly understood.

While national and international crises multiply, the media of communications continue to perfect the marvelous devices of press, radio, television, and now communication satellites, through which people throughout the world can learn about, and often actually see and hear, one another at work, at play, and in battle. Even the most primitive of our fellows has some contacts with the great world outside his village.

This breakdown of isolation and provincialism has brought us both nearer together and farther apart: nearer because, through the press and television, we are in daily contact with peoples of distant countries; farther apart because, seeing and hearing one another, we often misunderstand what we see and hear, owing to our ignorance of cultures other than our own.

Communications technology has revolutionized the practice of diplomacy. Governments still speak to other governments, but they speak also to peoples—and listen to them. As James Reston has pointed out, the mere fact that the President makes a statement or takes an action is news, and affects public opinion at home and abroad. Other, less prominent but more numerous, agents who influence public opinion, and hence the climate of international relations, are the idealistic Peace Corpsman, the long-suffering missionary, the foreign correspondent, the businessman, the visiting professor or student, and the propagandist. On their heels comes the survey researcher to analyze the state of public opinion on issues important to governments.

Meanwhile, modern social scientists in the field and in the universities have been accumulating a large body of knowledge concerning human behavior in different cultural settings, as well as a variety of techniques for measuring opinions, motives, and reactions, and sometimes even predicting group behavior. Social science has told us much about the basic drives of human action, probable reactions to a given stimulus, and the breaking points of human tension.

There have thus been at work for the better part of this century three streams of human endeavor which are beginning to come together. One is professional diplomacy, which, however, now uses many techniques unknown at the Congress of Vienna. Another is the new mass communications that bring the world within instant sight and sound, and thus form the basis of the new public diplomacy in which individuals and groups speak directly to one another across national boundaries—not always in the same accents as their governments. And there are the social scientists whose researches illuminate the wellsprings of human behavior, whether that of individuals, groups, or nations.

This book represents a pioneer effort to examine this relatively new phenomenon, the interaction of communications and the new diplomacy, in the light of the findings of behavioral science. Specialists in many fields—psychology, sociology, anthropology, public opinion, journalism, communications, and others—discuss what their respective disciplines can bring to the study of interpersonal and intergroup relations across national boundaries—and what the diplomat and the policy-maker can learn from their findings. Ten eminent authorities draw tentative conclusions on the potential of their professions or academic disciplines for informing diplomacy and making it a more efficacious force for good. A final essay considers the possibilities of convergence (and hence somewhat easier communication) between opposing social systems on either side of what is no longer an impenetrable iron curtain.

It was expected that experts of diverse experience might present conflicting testimony. While this occurred, it is significant that all of the authorities appeared to agree on the proposition that academic students of human behavior and private and official practitioners in the field of international relations would benefit by closer consultation with one another. In many cases understanding is impeded by the existence of esoteric vocabulary and concepts, in a few instances by one group's distrust of another's methods. At the same time, many of our authors recall instances of advantageous wartime or postwar collaboration; and, within the bounds of professional scruple and personal interest, all wish sincerely to share their experience and their problems with others engaged in the formation, the execution, and the analysis of public policy and international communication.

2

EDUCATIONAL AND CULTURAL RELATIONS

Charles Frankel

Columbia University
Former Assistant Secretary of State
for Educational and Cultural Affairs

Educational and cultural affairs are an important part of the current pattern of international relations, and offer instruments for diplomacy and foreign policy whose potential ability is enormous and has as yet only begun to be felt. But education and culture are not simply instruments of foreign policy; they are an essential part of what foreign policy today is all about. They enter into the definition of its ends and purposes and are not simply instruments for the achievement of ends that have been defined without regard to them. For we are in an era which has been fundamentally affected by certain new phenomena on the human scene, which have propelled educational and cultural relations to the forefront of international relations.

If I am right, we are entering an era that can properly be called "the era of educational and cultural relations." President Johnson's initiatives in this area, including his submission to the Congress of the International Education Act of 1966, are expressions of and responses to this era and efforts to stimulate a movement in our country which will help it to accommodate to what this era requires of it.

Educational and cultural relations between different peoples are, of course, not peculiar to our time. The first great epics in Western literature are devoted to the theme. The Trojan War appears to have been provoked by an excessively eager exercise in cultural exchange—the abduction of Helen. And the Bible contains one episode after another of cultural exchange, and a variety of comments about it. By failing to resist the temptation of the Serpent, Adam and Eve, after all, found themselves transported from the Garden of Eden to a quite different way of life. This is only the first in a long series of instances in which people have identified cultural exchange with the work of the Devil.

On a somewhat less cosmic level, we now have reason to believe that even before the Roman Empire laid out its roads there was an extraordinary commerce between East and West. Traces of pre-Roman Celtic civilization can be found from Britain to the Balkans.

Christianity, as we know, is a standing monument to cultural exchange. St. Paul was a Greek-speaking Roman Jew; St. Augustine moved in the course of his life from North Africa to Britain and sampled, among other points of view, Eastern Manicheism, Greek Skepticism, and Platonism. And at its high point medieval Christianity was enriched by the scholars, teachers, and students from many countries who gathered together at the great centers of Christian learning such as Paris.

Nor has cultural exchange been a purely intellectual or abstract phenomenon. As a result of Marco Polo's voyages, what we now know as spaghetti came to Italy, and the diet and economy of that country were substantially changed. Legend has it that coffee and croissants, that delectable combination, was one of the lasting contributions of the Turkish invasions of Europe. The croissant is the Turkish crescent. When the Turks were beaten back from the gates of Vienna in 1683, they left strange-looking green beans scattered around in their abandoned camps. They were coffee beans, and Vienna was never the same again. Whether this particular event is legendary or not, it does point to an important and unduly neglected truth; namely, that war has been one of the principal instrumentalities of cultural diffusion.

In the modern world, as we know, cultural exchange has become deliberate, planned, and widespread. The European nations for some centuries purposely transported their cultures, or bits of their cultures, to the colonial areas. And well-established nations like the Japanese and the Turks, in an effort to avoid being Europeanized at the direction of the Europeans, systematically sent their leaders and young people to various parts of Europe and North America, combing the West for ideas and techniques and adapting them to their own uses.

To speak of educational and cultural relations, then, is certainly not to speak of anything peculiarly new or contemporary. It is to speak of an aspect of human history that has been present from the time that different groups of human beings first came into contact with one another. These relations have been a consequence of war as well as of peaceful relations between human groups. A strong argument can even be made that most wars have been important in the long run only for the cultural exchanges they have initiated. In any case, whether in war or in peace, cultural exchange has been a major executive agent in the changes that constitute human history. An influential school of anthropologists has maintained, indeed, that contact with external cultures is the most important single cause—some have even insisted, the only cause—of the movement out of social inertia into social change.

Nevertheless, there is a difference, and a difference of the greatest significance, I believe, in cultural relations as we know them today. Broadly speaking, I venture to suggest, we may distinguish three great stages in the history of cultural exchange.

In the first stage, which covered the longest period in human history, cultural exchange was simply an accidental by-product of the contact between different groups. It was usually unsought, and it was frequently resisted.

In the second stage, cultural exchange—or, at any rate, the triumph of one's own culture over the culture of others—was not accidental, but was deliberately sought and promoted. It was a motive as well as a consequence of war, of commerce, of imperial organization and imperial rivalry; and the preponderant influence over it was exercised by government or government-sponsored activities or by churches. This is the period of the great explorations and of colonization, which came to its climax in the nineteenth century.

Characteristics of the New Era

The third stage is the one into which we have now entered. It is marked by an extraordinary flow of cultural traffic—of people, news, ideas, ideologies, fashions, machines, and passions—between almost all the human groups in the world. This cultural exchange, a good part of which is not deliberately planned or intended, goes farther and penetrates more deeply than any kind of cultural exchange known in the past. And while efforts can be and have been made to resist the flow of this traffic, it is probably not fundamentally resistible; it is an almost automatic consequence of changes in the character of human thought and work and in the conditions of human travel and communication. Most of us live in a physical, psychological, and moral neighborhood that has an international color and dimension, and we live in such a neighborhood whether we know it or not, or like it or not.

This is not all that characterizes this third, relatively new, stage in the history of cultural relations. Organized social institutions—churches, universities, foundations, voluntary associations, and governments—also play a heavier role than ever as initiators and regulators of the cultural traffic. In brief, in this third stage cultural exchange is the accidental but at the same time the inexorable consequence of the accelerating contact of heterogeneous human groups, and it is also deeply affected by deliberately adopted social policies, official and unofficial.

Finally, this cultural exchange has a new quality. Not only do the powerful nations impose themselves on the attention of the less powerful, but the less powerful impose themselves on the attention of the more powerful. A century ago, an untutored inhabitant of an Asiatic city would likely have been made sharply aware every day that there really was a Europe, but a worker in a European factory might well not have had the fact of Asia's existence clearly focused in his mind. Such ignorance is not common today. The flow of information, attention, and trouble is in both directions, and the flow is between cultures and peoples who have in the past regarded themselves as remote in history, experience, and destiny.

As in the case of any other so-called "stage" or "era" in history, we can, of course, trace the sources or prototypes of this new era to places and times fairly far back in the past. During the Middle Ages, the Catholic Church promoted the idea of a European culture that crossed over the mountains and transcended even the intense feudal loyalties of the period. To some extent, particularly through its support of learning, the Church promoted not only the idea but also its realization in practice.

In the postmedieval era, science and the organization of learned societies also fostered cultural exchanges, as did the gradual growth of the notion that humanists and scholars had a common vocation and a common audience. In the period of great imperial rivalries, artists, writers, philosophers, scientists, and students visited the great capitals of Europe. In the nineteenth century, at the height of the period of cultural imperialism, during which the richer nations moved out toward the poorer ones, a very powerful counter-tendency emerged in the form of a migration of the poor, perse-cuted, and unlettered from the Old World to the New.

Nevertheless, the most decisive characteristics of the new era of cultural relations have emerged only recently. In the present century, and particularly in the last twenty years, the internal history of every nation and the intimate daily experience of grow-ing numbers of individuals have been vitally affected by certain radical changes. Among these changes are the revolution in knowl-edge and in the place that the man of knowledge occupies in society, the extraordinary revolution in the technology of travel and communication, the advent of the school as a major instrument of social development and social control, and the rapid and now almost universal acceptance of the egalitarian language and moral outlook of democracy. Whatever the practice of a people or a government may be and however various or even bizarre their interpretations of democracy may seem, there is hardly a people or a government in the world today which would not try to explain and justify its behavior in democratic terms.

In these factors we have the major sources of the new era of cultural relations. They are of such magnitude that they imply a new era in international relations as well. They have changed the nature and conditions of national power, the character and function of diplomacy, and the very terms, I believe, in which the conception of "national interest" must be defined.

The Revolution in Knowledge

The revolution in knowledge, the first of the factors that affect the present scene, has had a number of significant consequences that are relevant to our discussion. In the first place, the massive development of science as a social institution—as a set of arrangements for acquiring, communicating, and assessing information—has advanced and solidified the growth of an international community of co-workers whose standards and temper of mind and, not infrequently, whose loyalties transcend purely parochial barriers. Given the existence of science, even if of nothing else, international affairs are not simply an arena of rivalry, disagreement, and misunderstanding. They are also an arena in which some men speak the same language, seek the same goals, and have worked out a rational procedure for the resolution of differences of opinion.

Moreover, these men of science have newly-acquired prestige and influence, for in the last few decades the traditional relationship between science and technology has been altered. In the past, major technological innovations, like the wheel, the compass, or the steam engine, were often developed without the immediate support of any large body of basic theoretical research. Often, these technological innovations themselves provided instruments and analogies which were used by scientists.

Today, however, basic theoretical research is the indispensable prerequisite for the overwhelming proportion of technological inventions. "Research and development" is a major component of a modern industrial establishment. The power of American industry, for example, probably turns largely upon our capacity to devote large numbers of people and large amounts of capital to basic research and development.

Science more than ever before, therefore, is an engine which drives human history along its imperfectly charted road. And with this change there has also come, quite naturally, a new role and influence for scientists and for their typical institutions like the laboratory and the university.

It is no longer possible, therefore, for any country that desires to prosper, and understands the conditions for such prosperity that must now be met, to ignore the peculiar demands and the peculiar mores of the learned community. And under the pressure of scientific standards of workmanship, these demands and these mores are becoming increasingly alike in all countries, increasingly transnational and international. Indeed, not the least of these demands is that the scientific communities of the different nations, if only in their own self-interest, must remain in touch with each other.

Moreover, we must not imagine that the changes which science has brought are only in the field of physical innovation. It is more than evident that the application of new technologies involves great changes in human behavior and the organization of society and that they demand a degree of flexibility and a capacity for quick adaptation on the part of the human animal beyond anything that has been demanded of him in the past. Indeed, many technical innovations are actually innovations in the field of human organization. The assembly line and traffic controls are only more obvious examples. And these changes in the ways in which human beings organize their joint ventures have come to be influenced increasingly by fundamental research in the social sciences.

It is true that we continue to depend much more on hunch, on ingenuity, and on folk wisdom in arranging our social affairs than we do in the physical sciences. Nevertheless, it is reasonably plain,

I think, that just as the complexities and pressures of modern life have been generated very largely by organized research, the answers to these complexities and pressures, if we find them at all, are also likely to come in large part from organized research. And because organized research is increasingly international in its methods and practical consequences, this means, in effect, that we have systematized and galvanized the process of cultural exchange.

I do not take this, however, to be an optimistic utterance. It defines a problem; it does not offer a solution. For we have a natural interest in maintaining diversity in the world. A great many people in a great many nations tend to resist modern innovations. A large number of them, because of the preeminence of the United States in science and technology, blame these changes on us, even though they are rather the products of a secular change in human knowledge and in the relation of man to his environment. Not least, technology makes trouble because it makes trouble so visibly and noisily and communicates its impact so quickly and so far.

Ease of Communication

The revolution in the technology of travel and communication is in itself a second major factor in the emergence of the new era in international affairs that I am attempting to describe. It has made the reporting of news itself a major influence on what actually happens. It has made foreign places realities at the breakfast table every morning. It has put the decision makers under extraordinary pressure to make decisions quickly and to make half a dozen at once. It has placed a premium on planning and on the capacity to deliberate carefully about hypothetical problems, because the chance to deliberate about real ones is generally likely to be short and not very sweet. And not least, it fosters the impression that we know what is going on, and why, in other places because we see and hear so much about them.

A particularly troublesome example of this may well be our present relations with Western Europe. The natural flow of people, information, and ideas between the United States and Western Europe may well encourage the belief in many people's minds on each side of the Atlantic that they have an accurate understanding of the other side. A reasonably large part of the news in European newspapers, for example, is devoted to the American domestic scene. But understanding does not consist in grasping isolated bits of information, numerous as they may be. It consists in knowing how to connect these bits and pieces of information, in being able to place them in the context that explains and illuminates them and guides us in drawing proper inferences from them.

This understanding in depth cannot be brought into being by a series of reports flashed out into the night. It requires a slower process of education, personal communication, and systematic discourse among those who have the greatest influence in shaping the fundamental categories and habits of thought of a population. Precisely because the peoples of the Atlantic area hear so much and see so much of each other, there is a strong necessity for systematic programs of educational and cultural exchange across the Atlantic. There is a job for schools and universities to do, and for teachers and students, and it is probably a larger job than before.

Role of the School in Social Development

The job of teachers, students, and educational institutions is perhaps even more evident when we turn to the developing nations. For it is plain, to begin with the most elementary fact, that if we are to have fruitful and mutually beneficial relations with the people of these nations, we must know more about them. Not enough of us know very much, and too many of us know nothing at all. That is why a basic element of the President's program in international education was the International Education Act of 1966, a proposal whose intention was to strengthen the intellectual capacity and cultural imagination which we Americans can bring to any of our activities overseas.

But an even more powerful imperative stands behind the steps that the U.S. Government is taking to sharpen and increase its efforts in international education. It is the imperative presented by a secular change in social structures of the greatest significance. The family, traditional religious organizations, and the neighborhood community have in the past been the most powerful social agencies with regard to the formation of human attitudes and the control of human behavior.

In both modern and modernizing societies, however, the power of these agencies must now be supplemented. They cannot by themselves cope with the pace of change or the disturbances of industrialization and urbanization. Neither are they capable of training people in the skills a modern economy requires or in the attitudes and national perspective which spell the difference today between a viable and unviable society. The school—primary, secondary, or advanced—has in consequence been projected to the forefront of contemporary history. It has become an indispensable agency of social development and control.

The school is fundamental in our foreign relations because investment in human beings is an indispensable investment for development. It is fundamental because education is not only a capital investment but provides a consumer's good which a mounting number of people everywhere are demanding with greater and greater urgency for themselves or their children. It is fundamental because only the school can provide individuals with the means to understand and control their experience with all the elements it contains that signal the existence and importance of distant places in the world.

Last but not at all least, the school is fundamental because close association between the schools of different countries is a primary means for creating, for the long run, patterns of mutual respect and forbearance on the international scene. The close relation of education to development has been emphasized by the President in messages to the Congress, and is reflected in the greater emphasis which the Agency for International Development is giving to education, along with health and food production, in its programs. But beyond the recognition of education as an instrument of development, there is an additional feature of the President's program that is equally important. Educational cooperation with other nations is conceived as part of the enduring national interest of the United States, a necessity for us and for others in building a firmer structure for peace.

The President's program addresses itself not only to the emergency situation of the developing nations but to an aspect or characteristic of the human scene today that is going to be present even if—and after—the problems of the developing nations begin to recede. It adds a new dimension to the Federal Government's interest in education. That is why an important responsibility for the program has been lodged in the Cabinet department which has the general and abiding responsibility for education—the Department of Health, Education, and Welfare.

Advent of Democracy

These considerations take me to the final characteristic of the present international scene which has pushed educational and cultural relations to the foreground. It is the advent of democracy and of the language of liberty, equality, and fraternity as the fundamental legitimation, real or professed, for contemporary government and for the struggles and aspirations of the inhabitants of this planet.

International affairs can no longer be conducted and no longer are conducted as affairs between the high and mighty, the crowned heads and elected presidents, alone. The heads of government speak over the heads of their fellows to the citizens who are the presumed source of authority. Every important move in foreign policy involves an effort not only to move another government but to move public opinion. And distant though public opinion may seem from the councils where the decisions are made, it has its effect, if not immediately, then in the long run.

In the long run, international educational and cultural relations play a decisive role in the formation of public opinion. They work perhaps less dramatically than the more rapid techniques for effecting changes in opinion, and these latter, of course, cannot be neglected. But opinion is generally a reflection of character and outlook, of long training and education, and not simply of the most recent information that one receives. If public opinion in our nation and in the world is to be consistent with the interests of peace and of mutual tolerance between diverse systems and cultures, a substantial effort must be made in the field of mutual education and cultural exchange.

It is, of course, possible to adopt alternative approaches to this state of affairs. At least once before, the nations of Europe were faced by a secular shift in the conditions of national security and power. This occurred when improvements in navigation made it possible for them to move out into the open seas. They met this test by establishing a system of commercial rivalry and warfare with whose effects we are still struggling. In the emerging era of

educational and cultural relations, the solidification of a system
of educational and cultural warfare and ideological recrimination
is of course a possibility. The school systems of the world, past
and present, have made their contributions to chauvinism and
insularity.

But there is an alternative. In an era in which men demand
equality, in which the citizens of nations long subject insist on
looking you in the eye, it is possible—and it is necessary—to seek
cultural exchange on a basis of equality and in the spirit that each
nation has as much to learn as to teach. It is possible—and it is
necessary—to act on the principle that, where education is concerned and where a people's deepest values are at issue, the ear as
well as the mouth should be brought into play.

Educational and cultural relations today, if they are to serve the
common causes of humanity and if they are to serve our most
enduring national interest, require a delicate touch and a cooperative international approach. They cannot rest on the presumption
that our nation or any nation has a mission to educate the world.

Guidelines for the New Era

Chaucer wrote of the clerk of Oxford: "And gladly wolde he
lerne and gladly teche." This is the spirit of the initiatives in
international education that have been launched by President
Johnson. They represent an effort on our part to make ourselves
ready for a cooperative enterprise in which we will join with other
nations, if they desire.

What are the basic guidelines for educational and cultural policy
in this emerging era of educational and cultural relations? They are
implicit, I think, in what I have said.

Educational and cultural programs should be bilateral or multilateral wherever possible, not unilateral.

They should rest on the established principle in all free educational systems that there is a difference between education and propaganda, and they must exemplify this principle in practice. Their success should be measured against long-term goals, not short-term ones.

They should be geared, for practical reasons as well as for reasons of policy, to the needs, interests, and modes of behavior of the people most immediately concerned: scholars, teachers, artists, students.

They should be conceived and implemented as continuing programs, as responses to imperatives that are now permanent on the human scene. They should not be viewed primarily as a means for the achievement of passing objectives.

Finally, the educational and cultural programs of the Federal Government, though they are indispensable, should properly be viewed only as elements in a larger national enterprise. They should not be and cannot be substitutes for nongovernmental efforts. Their main purpose, properly, is further to release and stimulate the energies of the non-Federal and private sectors of our country, which are already leading the effort in international education and cultural exchange.

The Test and the Opportunity

I confess that, as a man who has spent most of his life as a professional teacher of philosophy, I am tempted to ask the kind of troublesome question about the human aspects of international relations that has made philosophy notorious. For international relations, after all, are relations between nations, and nations are composed of human beings. Even diplomats probably qualify as members of the species. What can possibly be meant, then, by speaking of the human aspects of international relations as though there were some aspects of international relations that were not human?

But there is, of course, a meaning that can be given this question. There are those, past and present, who have held that relations between nations must be measured by principles that transcend human interests. They have insisted that states or nations are superior things unto themselves, whose significance and destiny are not meant to be measured by the fate of the individual human beings who compose them. And in this century as much as ever, and perhaps more than ever, the language in which foreign policy is justified has become increasingly abstract. Moreover, much of what we have known and still know as "foreign relations" is official and formal. It is not the kind of relation that individuals have to their immediate neighbors, and often the same rules do not seem to apply.

To speak of "the human aspects of international relations" is to call attention to what is unstructured and unformalized, to what is a matter of personal psychology or social outlook, and to the intercourse between individuals and groups in different nations that takes place because the people concerned want it to and not because the officials have said that it must. Educational and cultural relations are therefore a very large part of what we mean by "the human aspects of international relations." Today, an alert and responsive government cannot help but have a larger interest in them.

The dangers are plain. Government officials, even professors of philosophy on leave of absence, should be carefully watched at any time, and certainly when they suggest that they have an interest in matters that belong above all to private taste, judgment, and conscience, or to the free community of scholars and teachers. Yet a government policy in the field of international education and cultural exchange is an inescapable imperative today, as inescapable as a policy on defense or commerce or outer space. It is inescapable because there has been a change in the human environment. The response that a government gives to this imperative will test its alertness to new necessities and to something more besides. It will test its fidelity to a liberal view of human civilization. For, in the end, the free exchange of ideas, the free movement of people, the meeting of individuals as individuals without regard to the borders—none of these is simply an instrument of national policy. The national policy of a free and civilized government is one instrument for achieving such ideals.

In brief, we are well into an era in international relations that deserves to be recognized as qualitatively new. It will test government, but it will test a great many people who are not in government as well; and it will test the capacity of people in and out of government to work together. But it is more than a test; it is an opportunity to go farther with ideals that have lit the history of our civilization and to appreciate them more deeply.

There is, however, a somber, or at any rate a not entirely encouraging, aspect to the thesis I have put before you. If it is true that the era of educational and cultural relations implies that the human aspects of international relations will become even more pronounced than in the past, I am not sure that I have left you with an entirely reassuring thought. The only consolation I have to offer is that it would be even less cheerful to say to you that our future is not at all in our hands.

3

COMMUNICATION ANALYSIS AND COMPREHENSIVE DIPLOMACY

Bryant Wedge

Institute for the Study of National Behavior

The great acceleration in the flow of information across national boundaries during the last half-century, together with radical changes in the organization of international life, confront diplomacy with unprecedented challenges. The world has never been like this before; new thinking is demanded by new conditions of the human venture.

Fortunately, the sciences of human behavior have rapidly developed new and powerful methods to analyze and interpret the challenge to diplomacy. The organization and application of these methods constitutes the new profession of communication analysis.

It is still too early to define this new profession in detail, but it is possible to apply some basic concepts to interpret the diplomatic challenge and to illustrate the application of scientific principles to the analysis of specific cases of international communication difficulties.

National Reality Worlds

Every person carries in his mind a picture of the world—sets of assumptions and expectations by which he acts. We build these from repetitive experience. Fire burns, objects fall, rooms are rectangular, and so on. Once these assumptions are established they become the basis for action; indeed, our expectations are so strong and so persistent that we see the world in terms of them and so develop an outlook that creates its own reality. In daily life this permits us to act with some certainty and saves us from the madness of having to treat each new encounter afresh. Such assumptions are to a large degree automatic in daily life, but if one met cold fire, rising objects, or distorted rooms, a problem would be created which would require conscious attention and which would force us to make exceptions to our general rules. In fact, this is the only way we ever learn anything new.

Since each individual's experience is uniquely his own, the view of the world which he has is specific to him; it is his "unique reality world," as Hadley Cantril calls it.[1] This fundamental view of the world, built upon experience and carried into our transactions with the environment, also enters potently into our social and political expectations. We are able to deal with one another because we share certain conventions which we have learned by experience— conventions such as language, gesture, and habits of belief and value. The shared conventions of a people are the outcome of their collective history and circumstances; these become incorporated into the reality worlds of individuals. Thus, the repetitively rein-forced social assumptions of a people enter deeply into the outlooks of its individual members.

An understanding of these elementary facts of social psychology is essential if one is to grasp the persistent force of distinctive national viewpoints. The shared conventions, the habits of reason-ing and communication, the beliefs and loyalties which vary from country to country and which are inculcated and reinforced by every instrument of the modern national state, become internalized in the individual and determine his interpretation of reality. When we understand that national outlooks constitute *reality* as this is understood and agreed upon by national citizens, we have taken the first and longest step toward dealing with international inter-course in terms of the forces which actuate the behavior of nations and their representatives.

The adjustment of affairs between nations depends on bridging these differences in outlook in such a way that we truly understand the intentions of other nations and their leaders and make ourselves correctly understood by them. If, at the same time, we maintain a clear definition of our own role and position in international affairs, we should be able to reduce the friction and miscalculation which arise from misunderstanding, and secure workable international arrangements based on national self-interest. I submit that the adequate development and application of a science of international communication based on an understanding of comparative national psychology would contribute to effective policy formation and international transactions in the world, divided as it is.

Communication with Whom?

The various nations of the world are in differing phases of the political and psychological mobilization of their people. Their decision processes are influenced by one elite or another. Their national concerns are determined by their unique history and circumstances. The most effective channels and instruments of communication are therefore quite specific to any given nation, and the diplomacy suitable for dealing with that nation is determined by these specifics.

If communication is to be effective, it must be directed to those who have a significant voice in national decision-making. Insofar as it has ever been possible to locate national decisions in a single body, it has been in the legal "sovereign," whether this be a person, a government, or a party. Certainly such corporate representatives of nations are still highly influential, in a few cases almost absolute. The conduct of business between nations requires careful attention to the art of negotiation with the representatives of governments, especially, of course, with heads of state.

Classic diplomacy evolved in a Europe dominated by comparatively stable governments capable of speaking for their polities.[2] The ambassador, in these circumstances, requires secrecy and the confidence of his counterparts; he is especially concerned with national styles of statecraft.[3] In the practice of classic diplomacy, diplomats tend to acquire a common culture. They become more like each other than are the countries they represent.

Classic diplomacy and classic diplomats have been upset by two relatively recent developments. One of the most severe shocks in twentieth-century history was the discovery by Western diplomats that the Russians aren't "gentlemen." Americans during and after World War II were horrified to learn that a Russian official's signature on a Lend-Lease agreement was not binding, and that unsecured loans meant nothing to them. Lately, even the French have taken to acting very undiplomatically in terms of nineteenth-century methods.

The second change which appalls classic diplomatists is the rise of a multitude of "irregular" international dealings which affect classic negotiations. The modern national state is characterized by a diffusion of the decision process, and consequently of sovereignty, toward constituencies. This is the outcome of citizen participation in national tasks; participation sooner or later gives citizens a voice. Most important are the elites, the bureaucrats and technocrats, the men of ideas and the public press, the artists, and the managers. Ultimately, in advanced modernization, sovereignty comes to rest in the public, and leaders become the "servants of the people"; hence the growing importance of public opinion.[4]

What has been called the "new diplomacy" recognizes the diffusion of the decision process and applies broader criteria to the process of negotiation, tending to consider each of the channels of communication as a legitimate area for diplomatic endeavor.[5] Something of the complexity of modern international political communications, utilizing one or more of the twenty-eight channels in the model devised by Harold Sprout[6] (Figure 1), is outlined in W. Phillips Davison's latest book.[7] Davison points out that there are multiple media, from bags of wheat to Telstar, for conveying messages through these channels. It is no wonder that Davison recommends simplifying matters by creating a Freedom of Information policy for the United States. Indeed, such a policy, vigorously pursued, appears to be the only possible effective approach to broad-range international communication in the modern world.

Classic diplomacy (channel Ag-Bg in the Sprout model) remains important; but as our Secretary of State has learned in the Vietnam affair, activities in other channels affect those in this primary channel. Many of the more unusual channels have carried messages critical in our interpretation of the situation in Hanoi and, in the end, have been useful to a diplomatic service which resisted the use of such channels.

The practices of classic negotiation and the new diplomacy require different skills and attitudes. Both classic and new diplo-

FIGURE I

Channels of International Political Communication (Sprout)

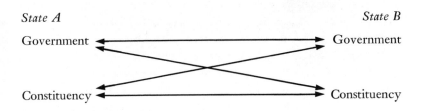

State A   State B
Government   Government

Constituency   Constituency

Uni-Directional Flow
  4 Primary Channels (Ag–Bg = Diplomacy, Ag–Bc, Ac–Bg, Ac–
    Bc)
  8 Secondary Channels (e.g., Ag–Bc–Bg = Information Programs,
    Ag–Ac–Bc, Ac–Bc–Bg, etc.)
 16 Tertiary Channels (e.g., Ag–Ac–Bc–Bg = Foreign Leader Ex-
    change, Ac–Ag–Bg–Bc, etc.)

macy have their place in the conduct of affairs between nations. A
comprehensive diplomacy would encompass both sets of skills in
the mixture appropriate to a given set of circumstances. Certainly,
the roles of negotiator and of public communicator are distinct
and often incompatible. Both roles and sets of skills are surely
weakened when there is confusion between them. Perhaps the full
development of *comprehensive diplomacy* will require two or
more different patterns of training and career to fully develop
specific diplomatic capabilities.

The Analysis of Communication Problems

Khrushchev supplied an elegant little example of communication
failure on his first visit to the United States. When he attempted to
convey the greetings of a brotherly people to his American audi-

ence by his gesture of the clasped hands of friendship waved about his smiling face, he failed to take account of American conventions. Photographs of the event in our newspapers were widely captioned to suggest his gesture as that of a victorious pugilist. Khrushchev failed to communicate as he intended, and our newspapers failed to interpret his intentions correctly.

Similarly, when John Foster Dulles delivered a brace of Western revolvers to Nasser as a gift from President Eisenhower during discussions of Egyptian requests to purchase arms from the United States, it is not hard to imagine that the intention of conveying personal greetings with a touch of Americana may have assumed a different significance in the Egyptian President's mind, especially when one considers the possibility of differences in interpretation of symbolic gestures by the two men and their respective cultures.

These little illustrations, which could be continued almost endlessly, suggest that, as Walter Lippmann wrote, "The failure to recognize that there are many worlds, not merely one, is the deepest source of confusion between us. . . ."[8] Indeed, when historiography begins to apply the concept of comparative outlooks to interpretation of international episodes, it may be found that misunderstandings of the most concrete and literal kind have played a large role in conflicts between nations.

Suppose, however, that it were possible to identify and correct such misunderstandings as they occur or, preferably, before they occur. In some cases this has been accomplished by systematic investigation of the way the other fellow sees us and interprets our actions. Once the sources of his "misinterpretation" of our intentions are identified, we are sometimes enabled to shape our messages to him in such a way as to convey a more correct impression.

Here I shall cite some examples of actual cases affecting policy or operations in which a professional approach to communication analysis has contributed something beyond informed judgment and intuition, which are the usual bases for national decisions and actions. But such systematic approaches to problems of international communication are in their infancy and have been only rarely and unsystematically applied.

The procedure I shall follow in these examples is to outline the foreign outlook on specific issues as this has been identified by systematic investigation through dialogue with selected representatives of the population, opinion polling, or examination of statements and actions. This outlook will be contrasted with the American viewpoint as it is generally understood; regrettably, it is difficult to examine United States premises and opinions in a systematic fashion. Then I will suggest how American presentations can be shaped so that our intentions may be more accurately understood. The process is simple in its essentials. The technical contribution of psychological science is in systematic identification and description of the various sources of misunderstanding and communication of these findings to the relevant policy communities, public or private.

CASE I

University students in Brazil in 1964 frequently confronted American visitors with the question, "Who killed Kennedy?" They immediately followed the question with their own answer, which was always a theory of conspiracy with more or less detailed "evidence." They held that "rightists"—a term encompassing the CIA, the Pentagon, the "steel barons," the John Birch Society, and "neo-imperialist capitalists"—were involved, sometimes in concert with Communist organs and agents, who, it was argued, have been known to make common cause with bourgeois elements. This question and answer are more important than they may at first appear, for wrapped up in the issue is a whole series of preconceptions about the United States.

As I listened to the discussion and followed its reasoning, several characteristics became apparent. First, their theory rested on the assumption that the political system in the United States was similar to that of Brazil: a privileged elite exercising disproportionate power and refusing to yield to legal discipline, and a radical minority, purporting to represent the interests of the common people, using any means to reach its ends. Second, students argued on the basis of a preconceived theory and perceived all evidence in the light of this. For example, the publication of excerpts from the report of the President's Commission on the Assassination of President Kennedy did not affect their view in the slightest; in reading the Appendix on "speculations and rumors" these students had a striking tendency to accept the speculations as evidence and to ignore the discrediting material altogether or to classify it as a labored whitewash. Finally, there was a strong tendency toward emotional association; President Kennedy was literally loved and anyone who was believed to have opposed any of his policies was despised and believed capable of evil. Furthermore, they completely discredited official and printed evidence, especially if it came from the United States.

Americans, of course, had been vitally concerned with the same question and had certainly considered the possibility of conspiracy. But the response was different, and typically American. Our approach was to gather, examine, and test the evidence in laborious detail. Having concluded, on the basis of facts, that the assassination was the act of a madman acting alone, we tried to communicate our conclusions. We failed completely with these students, for we expected them to give the same weight to evidence as we did.[9]

In over seventy instances of extended dialogue with groups and individuals on this subject, I found that efforts to argue from the evidence had no effect; students would oppose my "facts" with "facts" of their own, often of the most far-fetched nature, but they would also argue logically from their firmly held theories of

American society that there *must* have been a conspiracy. Such contrast in patterns of reasoning and argument appeared in many efforts at dialogue between Americans and Brazilian students. Americans, in their frustration, tended to resent the Brazilian's stubborn suspicion of evidence. Brazilian students, for their part, did not find American styles of logic credible; students on exchange visits, for example, listening to distinguished American professors building generalizations from evidence, have concluded that "Americans don't know how to think."

This kind of communication failure is *not* based on national hostility but does result in scornful and suspicious attitudes on each side toward the other national culture. Secondary rationalizations for the failure to communicate occur on both sides, often in the form of suspicion. Americans may consider the breakdown in communication to be evidence of "Communist" indoctrination; Brazilians may feel that they are the objects of "imperialist" pressure. The reactions certainly contribute to acts and policies on both sides which complicate relations.

Once a source of communication failure is recognized, efforts can be made to correct the problem. In this case, it was possible to experiment with variations in the presentation of the American viewpoint in actual dialogue with students and to test their reception. It should be noted that no alteration of the position was necessary. Two approaches, based on an understanding of what "makes sense" to Brazilian students, proved to be effective. The first involved confronting the conspiracy theory with another theory—a general theory of assassination motives. It was argued that important figures may assume symbolic value in the eyes of envious and mentally disordered persons and become the objects of their attack. Brazilian students are fascinated with psychological theory, and there was enough evidence of such disturbance in the assassin's personality to back the thesis. The gratifying outcome of several such dialogues was that the students introduced theory and examples from their own national experience. In Brazil, it proved more effective to counter a theory with another theory than with facts.

The second adaptation of presentation to the audience involved the use of emotional association. Instead of discussing the evidence of the Warren Commission, we discussed the personality of the Chief Justice. Most Brazilian students associate Chief Justice Warren with social justice, and especially with the popular school desegregation decision. By establishing such acceptable bona fides and then pointing out that the popular and incorruptible Chief Justice had headed the investigation and had endorsed its conclusions, the evidence, which had been doubted on its own ground, became more credible.

Americans, in their own society, are suspicious of theory and of the authority conveyed by personality. We tend to feel that facts should speak for themselves and that every man should judge the evidence. Since contrasting patterns of reasoning exist in Brazil, it is no wonder that American argument often fails to convey its intended meaning. But it does no violence to American convictions to respect the requirements of the Brazilian patterns of reasoning, and we are often forced to do so in order to make ourselves understood. In this case, demonstration of the Brazilian's characteristic mode of reasoning has led to some changes in our understanding of statements made by Brazilian students and in our presentation of information to them by government and private agencies. For example, American professors can adduce their evidence in terms of deductive reasoning from broad principles and thus become more understandable to Brazilian student audiences.

CASE II

A second illustration concerns a more specific case: Soviet-American negotiations on disarmament. In order to grasp Soviet attitudes and intentions on this subject, the verbatim record of the Eighteen-Nation Conference at Geneva was systematically studied and a model of Soviet assumptions and concerns expressed therein was constructed.[10] Once again, radical contrasts with American approaches were evident. The Soviets continually insisted upon agreement to principles first; the details were then supposed to fall into place. The Americans consistently held that technical details had to be settled before they would accede to a broader agreement. One manifestation of this difference was the relative attention given to scientific data: the United States constantly consulted technical experts and advocated expert conferences to settle these issues; in the Soviet view, these actions had political, not practical, motives. The Soviets invented the term, "the scientific screen," to describe our attempt to apply technical criteria in political negotiations.

There are a number of such contrasts in the negotiation, but a particularly difficult problem arose from the Soviets' persistent approach to the negotiations as an occasion for political bartering. The Soviet Government and its negotiators evidently perceived the negotiation in a broad political context, and drew in issues and made proposals which appeared quite peripheral to the matter at hand. It was noted that such proposals were often coupled with responses to United States suggestions and it was hypothesized that this represented a covert attempt at political barter, suggesting willingness to consider an American proposal in return for some concession on a matter of interest to themselves. On examination, this hypothesis proved to be thoroughly consistent with patterns of doing business and international dealings in the Russian culture.

The American negotiators, of course, considered the conference to be concerned only with the issue at hand—progress toward disarmament—and were only prepared to discuss arrangements within the confines of that issue. To the Americans, the Soviets seemed to be making propaganda moves, attempting to evade the issues, or trying to gain political advantage. It was certainly difficult to believe that the Soviet negotiators were making serious efforts to exchange what they believed to be a political advantage for a disarmament step which they considered of strategic advantage to the United States. It is difficult to arrive at agreement when the parties have different views of what the negotiation is about.

In this case the American negotiators seriously considered the hypothesis that the Soviets were trying to barter on the model of (covert) counter-offer, better known as "Yankee horse-trading." This hypothesis was more strongly confirmed by the open offer made by Mr. Khrushchev in May 1963 to exchange a partial test-ban treaty for a nonaggression pact—a proposition which had been identified as a covert offer in analysis of the Geneva Conference. American willingness to explore the offer, strange as it may have seemed, depended on their ability to take seriously the Soviet techniques of obtaining agreement without, of course, yielding concessions on matters of substance. Obviously, accuracy of communication between cultures does not automatically bring agreement, but it is a necessary condition for arriving at viable agreements.

CASE III

A third illustration touches on a global problem in communication. Many statements and actions of a nation have world-wide impact and are variously interpreted by other nations. One such problem concerns the image of our nation's political and economic system which is conveyed by, among many other things, the words which we use to describe ourselves.

As Ralph White has shown in his brilliant essay on " 'Socialism' and 'Capitalism': An International Misunderstanding," much of the world unequivocally regards the United States as "capitalistic."[11] While at first thought this may not be disturbing to Americans, an examination of the connotations attached to these terms by a very large proportion of the world's people reveals that distressing misconceptions of the United States are concealed in the words. To them, "capitalism" involves overtones of exploitation of men and of nations, while "socialism" suggests social justice and government restraint of economic rapacity.

The idea of the United States as "capitalistic" has done untold damage to the understanding of our country and its motives in international affairs. A typical argument among intellectuals from developing nations, for example, asserts that American assistance to agricultural development represents "economic neo-imperialism, a plan to keep us in a condition of economic servitude by extracting our wealth while resisting the industrial development which could make us more self-sufficient." Such arguments immensely complicate efforts to assist these nations by rational economic planning. The ramifications of this view and its consequences for relations with other countries are very extensive and largely inimical.

Americans, of course, tend to associate "socialism" with Communism and dictatorship, as well as with government ownership of the means of production; consequently, we do not readily assert our "socialism." But we do stand for social justice and have developed extensive means to forward its realization in our own country. We have long regulated private economic life and have evolved the world's fairest system for the distribution of income. We know this but we have obviously failed to convey either the fact or the commitment. It is no wonder that many visiting leaders from developing countries have been astonished at our "socialism."[12] The fact is that we have already achieved a level of social and economic justice to which many leaders of other nations who call themselves "socialists" aspire.

Lest this appear too easy to correct, I must also report that a substitute term, "free enterprise," is also subject to misinterpretation, as among some Latin Americans who believe that we insist on "the freedom of the fox in the chicken-coop." There *are* many ways to correct this misunderstanding once it is recognized, principally by describing and showing other people what we actually are through a process which ideally would involve every communication channel, especially that of private business overseas. White and I, among others, have made a number of concrete suggestions, many of which are gradually being realized, but it is particularly important that we avoid the reinforcement of the image by continued use of these ambiguous terms. I am glad to report that this has been understood for some time at the highest policy levels of the United States government and policy statements have been framed in terms of this understanding.

CASE IV

As a final example, I will mention an act of policy. The ill-fated multilateral force proposals of our government seemed to us to be a sensible way to both share and control nuclear force. It was argued that this would assure our adversaries of our nonaggressive intentions while presenting them with a credible deterrent in Europe and that it would satisfy and reassure our allies. In fact it did neither, for each interested country viewed the proposal in terms of its specific outlook. To mention only two, the Soviet Union feared that MLF represented a step toward German possession of nuclear weapons; it reacted vigorously and could not be reassured, for Russia has what may be called a traumatic fixation on German "militarism." France, or at least de Gaulle, saw the offer as an attempt to "subordinate" her to American hegemony and also reacted with a vigorous No.

It is true that there were also good reasons of power politics for France and Russia to object to this policy. I believe that the

American policy was instituted in full knowledge of these political factors, but that there was a complete failure to recognize the deep psychological roots of the reaction which took place and which has done very serious damage to the process of détente which we seek as an official policy and to the process of European integration which we also seek to encourage.

It took the United States some time to recognize that, however we saw the proposal, the other countries saw it differently and could not be persuaded to our views. In this case, too, a *tour d'horizon* of how other countries perceived our proposal helped stimulate a reconsideration of its utility.[13]

One can only speculate as to whether such consideration could have been made before the proposals were put forward. Some defense policies are being considered in such terms before they are announced, at least experimentally; the suspicion has grown that cost-effectiveness, national strategic models, and even conventional power-politics models are insufficient bases on which to predict international response.

A Science of Cross-Cultural Communication

The fragments of case studies which I have offered are the outcome of the deliberate and somewhat laborious application of techniques of systematic analysis to specific problems. These techniques rest on a body of social science theory and method; here we enter into a technical and specialized field.

One example of a technical approach to the analysis of a communication problem was provided by a study of distinctive patterns of reasoning and argument among Brazilian students. In this case an appreciation of the role of cognitive styles in communication was indispensable to the identification of the problem. Edmund Glenn and I have developed a cognitive matrix which, in its simplest form, permits us to describe twenty-five distinct patterns of logic and reasoning; we have identified these patterns in a number of instances of national discourse with respect to specific national issues.[14] (Figure 2.)

At the top of the vertical axis is the term "universalism," which we have applied to the mode of reasoning predominant among Brazilians, for whom global, idealistic theory determines to a very high degree the perception of any kind of evidence. At the bottom of the vertical axis is "case-particularism," which characterizes American thinking; we pay closer attention to the evidence and settle each case independently.

On the horizontal axis the term "association" refers to ideas and images bound together in one's mind because of their proximity in time or space. For example, Brazilians may say, "Gilberto Freyre is a bad scientist because he is a notorious conservative." We learn language and multiplication tables by associative thinking. As we mature intellectually, we move away from association toward abstraction. We Americans shift our cognitive styles depending on the subject we're dealing with; but in terms of international political argument the United States probably lies between the rational and abstractive positions on the horizontal axis of this scale.

The Dominican Republic is placed in the lower left-hand corner of the matrix. I have found young Dominican revolutionists to be the most actively oriented-to-evidence people I have ever met. They are so profoundly concerned with taking things case by case that they have difficulty in building generalizations. I am sure that this is related to the difficulty Dominicans have in developing cooperation among themselves; they can't find superordinate or common generalizations they can agree on. One of the consequences is that the grapevine among Dominicans is remarkably accurate.

I have hypothesized that this pattern of thinking tends to de-

FIGURE 2

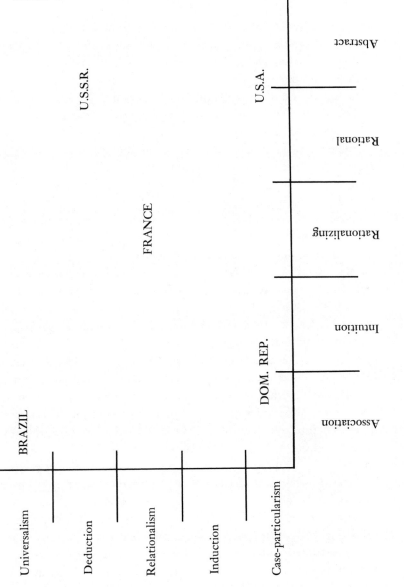

velop in cultures dominated by police-state political methods; in such circumstances, survival may depend upon having the facts straight. And the Dominican Republic has had a long history of brutally suppressive governments. Similar factual particularity has been observed among students in East Berlin.

The identification of the most common or modal pattern of thinking and social discourse among a given population is based on the analysis of the styles of argument and presentation which are normally used in attempting to teach or convince others. Such observations may be made in the classroom, in dialogue, and by analysis of written documents.

A nation's modal position on this scale has extensive implications for communicators and diplomats. Statements and actions of Dominicans may have quite different implications from those of similar statements made by Brazilians. I was able to predict, for example, that Dominican students would prove relatively resistant to the universalistic appeals of Marxist theory and would prove more responsive to practical considerations than persons who live in more universalistically-oriented societies. Moreover, it was predictable that the association of young democratic revolutionaries with Communist personalities would not necessarily imply a broader loyalty than practical purpose and would tend to cease when such causes were eliminated. In short, the claim of "revolutionaries" during the recent civil strife—that the presence of Communists did not make the revolution Communistic—accorded with Dominican psychology. Similar claims in other societies might not be credible. Subsequent history of the revolutionary movement has, so far, tended to bear out these predictions.

While a good deal of work remains to be done in refining and validating such instruments as the cognitive matrix, it appears that these instruments may have considerable potency in the analysis and prediction of political developments. Such findings may be valuable to the diplomat and the policy maker in determining the desirability of alternative courses of action.

Moreover, such instruments contribute to an understanding of the style and order of reasoning which may be necessary if American statements are to be correctly understood by other nations. A final example may suffice. The Soviet and United States modal styles are characterized by similar levels of abstraction but the order of presentation tends to be reversed; Russians reason from the general to the particular, Americans from fact to generalization. It is relatively simple to adapt to this contrast once the problem is recognized, yet many negotiations toward agreements desired by both sides have stumbled on this point.

In other examples given, use was made of techniques of opinion measurement, differential semantic analysis, the analysis of bargaining practices and of national interest perception. None of these tools is yet perfected, but crude as they are, they have already contributed to the identification and correction of some causes of international misunderstanding. The systematic application of the concepts and methods of the social and behavioral sciences, combined in a comprehensive approach to problem-solving in international communication, could result in the rapid development of a problem-solving science of cross-cultural communication analysis and, incidentally, the rapid improvement of the analytic technologies.

As in the development of medicine or engineering, such a profession would draw on a variety of scholarly and scientific resources and mobilize them to specific practical purposes. It would recruit concepts, methods, and even personnel from relevant fields; anthropology, history, linguistics, political science, psychology, sociology, philosophy, the technology of opinion measurement, and the new profession of public relations are among those which have already made distinct contributions.

Individual scientists from these fields, working in various universities and centers of communication study, have made individual contributions to communication problem-solving. Schools concerned with diplomacy and statecraft have sponsored some research and teaching in the field. Some public and private agencies engaged in international dealings have experimented with problem-solving studies. But each of these developments is rather unsystematic; none approaches the problems in a full-scale, problem-centered way. I believe that it is possible and highly desirable to define such a profession and to undertake research and training of professional specialists in the field of communication analysis. So far, the analyses of communication problems have been conducted from within scientific disciplines, which automatically restricts their method, or from professional positions such as that of diplomat, which automatically limits their scope.

The profession envisioned here would render services to the *practice* of cross-cultural communication; these include the refinement of useful theory and techniques, and problem-solving study in specific cases of communication difficulty. It is necessary here to draw a sharp distinction between the roles of communicator and of communication analyst.

International communicators include all those persons who exercise their professions in direct relation to other countries. These include the professional diplomat with his functions of representation and negotiation, the military men, educators, economists, businessmen, newsmen, and technical experts who operate in the international field. Each of these professions entails specific roles and responsibilities which are its primary concern, but knowledge and skill in cross-cultural communication is often vital to their effective fulfillment.

The analyst of cross-cultural communication is professionally concerned with the communication process itself; he has no role or responsibility other than the practice of his specialty. He is specifically *not* a communicator nor a policy-maker, but a technical expert and advisor. He would provide the tools for other professionals to use. Such a relationship exists between the economic analyst and economic policy-makers, and their productive relationship depends on keeping clear the distinction of role. There are two principal reasons for this: the role requirements of research and operational functions are frequently incompatible, and the technical tasks of research are too specialized and time-consuming for the operating professional to master and apply, in the face of his numerous professional responsibilities.

Confusion between these roles has decidedly impeded the development of skills and practices which would improve international communication. The diplomat is suspicious of investigators who may upset his mission or make policy recommendations, and rightly so. The social scientist, unless he is very clear about his function, is apt to confuse communication with policy. What is necessary to progress in this vital field is the clear definition of role and function and mutual respect for professional responsibilities that have been achieved in other fields which require the cooperative endeavor of specialists in solving complex problems.[15]

These issues are not just theoretical. My personal experience in this field has involved mistakes on both sides: I have offered policy recommendations which weren't asked for and have been asked for suggestions beyond my competence to give. Research findings have been taken as policy recommendations and have been criticized on policy rather than on evidential grounds. But an increasingly clear understanding of respective competences has grown out of this difficult experience and my services as communications analyst have been utilized with increasing effectiveness. The role considerations outlined above have grown out of this experience and out of a mutual interest in solving very real problems.

The Application of Cross-Cultural Communication Analysis

The systematic application of a science of cross-cultural communication would involve research, training, and problem-solving activities. Since this is an applied science, all of these activities should be directed to the development of a practical and teachable body of knowledge and skill which can be made available to international communicators.

I have outlined the most fundamental theoretical propositions: each individual perceives, thinks, and acts in terms of assumptions built into him by his experience, and groups of individuals organized into political bodies tend to share common assumptions. But the understanding of specific national modes of perception, reasoning, and action on the international scene requires detailed study; it is the function of research to develop and refine the concepts and techniques of the field.

Training needs to be conducted on two levels: the training of professionals in communication analysis and the training of international communicators, whatever their profession, in the general concepts and methods. Professional training would be intensive and technical; it would involve supervised field research and it would develop a cadre of professional specialists who could work in various agencies and schools concerned with international relations. Training of professionals in other fields would be designed to provide them with practical concepts and skills useful in their professional functions in cross-cultural settings and to acquaint them with the use of specialized resources available to them for the resolution of communication difficulties.

The problem-solving function has been illustrated by the cases presented above; in each case the studies were requested by the operational agencies and the findings were used by them to further their objectives. There is nothing new about this; specialists are often called in by organizations to help with technical problems. What is new is the recognition of specific communication problems and the use of communication analysis as such. In fact, the evidence reveals that such problems are more readily recognized when it is known that such resources are available.

It is not necessary to specify the agencies and enterprises which could benefit by the application of a science of cross-cultural communication; essentially, this encompasses the whole range of international communicators. The current problem is less one of identifying the uses of such a profession than of developing the profession to respond to recognized and pressing needs.

Concern for national security and the welfare of our society impels us to transcend a purely national viewpoint in order to communicate with others. This is the practical solution to the paradox of global interdependence and national dependence. A scientific profession of cross-cultural communication analysis represents the kind of social invention which could implement this solution and permit us to better understand and deal with other peoples in terms of their own national psychology without losing sight of our own.

4

PUBLIC OPINION RESEARCH

Lloyd A. Free

Institute for International Social Research

The assumption that public opinion is somehow important in international relations is borne out by the efforts of political leaders to woo it and by the practices of governments.[1] Every major government in the world today, and many of the minor ones, spend varying amounts of time, attention, and money on attempting to influence opinions on international matters among citizens of their own and other countries.[2] Oddly enough, judging from the colossal efforts they expend on propaganda at home and abroad, the modern totalitarian governments—from Hitler to Nasser to Communist Russia and China—are the most fervent believers of all in the idea that public opinion really counts.

In related vein, there has been a tendency in the case of at least some governments to give increasing attention to public opinion poll results, both domestic and foreign. Most of our recent American Presidents have been in the vanguard in this respect. Franklin D. Roosevelt was our first President to profit from really scientifically conducted polling. Particularly after the adverse reactions to his famous "Quarantine" speech, he was determined not to get too far out in front of public opinion concerning this country's participation in World War II—nor to stay too far behind. In this connection, he followed the polls with great interest, particularly trends of American public opinion charted for him by my associate, Hadley Cantril.[3]

Truman was much less oriented toward polls and polling; but I know from my own experience that President Eisenhower was deeply interested in the opinions of people in other countries. While working with Nelson Rockefeller in the White House as a consultant to the President in 1955, we started a series of periodic reports to Eisenhower on the psychological situation abroad, based chiefly on data gathered by the research branch of the United States Information Agency (USIA) under the able supervision of Leo P. Crespi. On one or two occasions, after John Foster Dulles had given one of his masterful briefings, the President was heard to say: "But you forget the human side, Foster," pulling out one of my reports.

It was during the Eisenhower years that one of my privately sponsored surveys scored a major success: a study in Japan covering not only public opinion, but attitudes of the four groups of greatest importance in the power and influence structure. Later, I learned that my report had actually received consideration at the level of the National Security Council; and President Eisenhower's then special assistant for national security affairs told a friend of mine that it was one of the most useful documents the NSC had had available during the time of his service there.

John Fitzgerald Kennedy was, of course, a fervent believer in polling. He not only depended heavily on Louis Harris's findings about domestic opinion, but followed closely the USIA data on opinion abroad. In the aftermath of the Bay of Pigs fiasco, USIA's findings—that Castro was little known in Latin America and was generally viewed by the public with considerable antipathy—contributed to the Kennedy Administration's adopting a relatively low-keyed approach to Castro and Castroism.

When it comes to that practitioner of "consensus," Lyndon Baynes Johnson, the picture is much the same. He regularly uses Oliver Quayle to poll in the United States on questions including international issues (Vietnam, for example), and keeps close at hand a thick, loose-leaf notebook not only of the latest surveys taken at home by Quayle, Gallup, Harris, and others, but also of polls conducted abroad.

Following the American intervention in the Dominican Republic in 1965, I immediately sent to the White House a report I had prepared in June of 1962 on the *Attitudes, Hopes, and Fears of the Dominican People*.[4] This showed that the Dominicans, as of then at least, were *the* most pro-American, anti-Communist, anti-Castro people we had found in any part of the world. Not only did President Johnson read the report, but the White House had it duplicated and distributed at the highest levels, and found it "very helpful." I have little doubt that it was one of the many factors which caused the Administration quickly to shift from an initial policy of exclusive support for the military junta to the later one of working toward a coalition solution.

Nor is this interest in public opinion surveys peculiarly American. Professor Stoetzel and Mlle. Riffault of the Institut Français d'Opinion Publique, for example, report that their results on political matters are regularly followed by President de Gaulle and the French government. Professor Noelle-Neumann of the Institut für Demoskopie in West Germany says that their data are sent to the Federal Government about twice a month and have a steady influence on the way it reports in its press conferences. A number of the Ministries of the Indian government, including External Affairs, are regular subscribers to the Monthly Public Opinion Surveys of Eric da Costa's Indian Institute of Public Opinion. The Japanese government has conducted its own polls on diplomatic problems, mainly the China issue, normalization of relations with Korea, and relations with the Soviet Union. The West German, British, French, and Indonesian governments, among others, have commissioned various studies abroad.

Foreign Office Myopia

There is another side to this story, however, much less pleasing to those interested in public opinion research. It has to do with the built-in "blind spots" toward the psychological aspects of world affairs exhibited by foreign offices and diplomatic corps the world over. For the most part, this includes our own State Department, and particularly, most of its older officials high in the pyramid of power and influence. The late, great John Foster Dulles once remarked: "If I so much as took into account what people in other countries are thinking or feeling, I would be derelict in my duty as Secretary of State." More than one American ambassador has, explicitly or implicitly, echoed the words of one of his colleagues—a career man—who said, while serving in a country that is now in a state of acute crisis, largely because of the turbulence of its public: "To hell with public opinion and public opinion polls. I am here to deal with the government, not with the public."

In other words, many if not most of at least our older State Department officials and Foreign Service officers continue to believe, in their heart of hearts, that the game of diplomacy can still be played as it was in the days before World War I. They do not include in their calculations the degree to which the public all over the world has, in fact, got into the act; nor the extent to which propaganda, popular persuasion, and information and cultural programs have become major instruments of the new diplomacy.

This insensitivity sometimes leads to very pertinent public opinion research findings being either neglected or ignored. The most cataclysmic such failure in my own experience had to do with the Bay of Pigs invasion. A year before, I had managed by the skin of my teeth to get a public opinion study done in Cuba.[5] This showed that Castro, at that time at least, was overwhelmingly popular among the Cuban people. There was a small opposition, but it was confined almost entirely to the city of Havana. Thus, whatever the expectations of those who planned the invasion, it came as no surprise to us that there was no popular uprising to assist the Bay of Pigs invaders. As with all of our reports, this study had been made available to the government, as well as to the public, and had actually been sent up to the White House by the bureaucracy. However, between the time our report was issued and the time of the attempted invasion, there had been a change of Administration when Kennedy came into the White House. And our findings were not called to the attention of the new President nor anyone on his staff when the question of invading or not invading was being considered.

Does "World Opinion" Really Exist?

Not long ago, another of our great Secretaries of State, Dean Acheson, claimed that Americans have a "Narcissus psychosis": "An American is apt to stare like Narcissus at his image in the pool of what he believes to be world opinion." After making the point that the only honest answer people in the world generally could give to questions on specifics of foreign policy would be a "don't know," he concluded, "World opinion simply does not exist on matters that concern us. Not because people do not know the facts—facts are not necessary to form opinion—but because they do not know the issues exist."[6]

Thus, we practitioners of the art of public opinion research are faced with some very basic questions: Does such a thing as "world opinion" exist? Do people in various parts of the world really have meaningful opinions on international issues? If so, are these opinions of importance to international relations? Replying to these questions is difficult and complicated; in fact, few generalizations can be made. The real answer is, it all depends.

To start with, I must define in my own way some of the terms we will be talking about. An opinion, in my terminology, is simply an expressed attitude, an attitude that is communicated. An attitude, on the other hand, is really a form of perception—a way of looking at a given subject. In the course of our lives, we build up all sorts of assumptions through experience in attempting to achieve our purposes; and these assumptions vitally condition what we perceive as the realities of the world in which we live. Our attitudes spring from this "reality world" or "assumptive world" of ours; they are the result of an interplay of our assumptions, shaped and modified by experience. If I can use a term very much overworked these days—"image"—an image is a rather fixed pattern of assumptions brought into operation by a situation in which one finds it necessary to react.

Hence, in a very real sense, if an individual has no assumptions learned from experience concerning a given subject or capable of being related to that subject, he can have no attitudes—and hence no opinions, let alone anything that might be denominated an image. And any opinions an individual may express will be *meaningful* if, and only if, he in some way relates the subject at issue to his own purposes, no matter how narrowly individualistic or broad these may be. The range of his sense of purpose is again delimited by his "reality world."

Every nonpsychotic individual on earth, no matter how primitive, has assumptions based on experience, and hence attitudes about *something*, even if they pertain only to his own personal life, his family, or his village. And he will relate many of these attitudes to his own purposes; so, he will have a certain fund of meaningful opinions which he can express, if—and this is a very important "if"—*you ask him the right questions*. Conversely, every individual in the world has his "blind spots" of greater or lesser scope; that is, subject matter areas in connection with which he has *no* assumptions to bring to bear, and hence about which he has no attitudes.

The Illiterates and the Ignorant

Let me illustrate from a study our Institute did in Brazil a few years ago.[7] When our interviewers asked rural Brazilians, most of whom are illiterate, about their *personal* aspirations in terms of their own lives, only 12 per cent were unable to respond. When the canvass was broadened to aspirations for their *country*, the "don't knows" jumped to one-third. The "reality worlds" of that proportion were not broad enough to extend to the nation as a whole. The moment the inquiry shifted to the international scene, almost all of them were left behind. Eight out of ten could not name any country with which Brazil should cooperate. Ninety-five per cent were unable to identify the President of the United States. Under the circumstances, it would be an exercise in sheer futility to ask these people questions about the specifics of foreign policy.

And this is a situation of world-wide dimensions. As President Johnson pointed out not long ago: "Today, more than 700 million adults—four out of ten of the world's population—dwell in darkness where they cannot read or write. Almost half of the nations of this globe suffer from illiteracy among half or more of their people."

Lest Americans cockily assume that this problem of ignorance about international matters is confined to the underdeveloped countries, let me cite from a study[8] that I conducted here in the United States, after the 1964 presidential election, on the political beliefs and values of Americans. From some questions designed to test information and knowledge, it turned out, for example, that only 43 per cent of Americans could identify U Thant and only 15 per cent Sukarno; that 25 per cent had never heard or read of NATO; and that only 41 per cent knew that Russia is not a member of NATO.

Looked at in this perspective, one can begin to see the validity of certain aspects of Dean Acheson's views, and to question, as W. Phillips Davison did in the *Public Opinion Quarterly*,[9] the common assumption among Americans that if enough people are persuaded to adopt a given opinion, then the policy of their government will be affected, at least in a democracy.

Publics: Limited and Mass

Before we write off the importance of public opinion in international relations, however, let us introduce some other aspects of the problem. To start with, every country in the world, no matter how primitive, has *some* people, no matter how small the proportion, who do have meaningful opinions about international matters —at least in regard to issues they feel are related to their nation's purposes. This group, in extreme situations of underdevelopment, may be limited, to all intents and purposes, to those in the gov-

ernment who have responsibility for conducting the foreign affairs of their country. Usually, however, it extends at least to a
broader educated elite, which may be of lesser or greater size.[10]
We thus come to the concept of the "informed public." The fact
that this elite may be small does not derogate from its power; we
can meaningfully define "world opinion" in terms of the opinion
of the publics which count in the particular situation, whether
limited or mass.

Beyond this, however, the broader public, or elements of the
public, can and often do get into the act, even in the underdeveloped countries. They may be "ignorant"; they may lack meaningful opinions on specific international issues. But at certain times
and places, their broader basic or implicit assumptions or images
may come into play in such fashion as to make a given issue,
fraught with international consequences, a matter of *public* concern. Often this applies only to a minority of the greater public;
frequently their concern is whipped up and organized for ulterior
ends, whether by the Communists or by local leaders. But *react*
they do; and often *act* they do.

This action may be as peaceable as signing a petition or writing
a letter to one's Congressman or the editor. But increasingly, more
extreme manifestations of public action in the form of demonstrations, picketing, and rioting—reflecting strongly held attitudes by
at least segments of the public—have become a phenomenon of
world-wide scope. For example, rioting in Japan and Korea made
it exceedingly difficult for the two governments to normalize their
relations. Demonstrations and rioting in Panama were unquestionably instrumental in causing the United States—after a decent in-
terval, of course—to agree to revise the Panama Canal Treaty.
Anti-Communist violence in Indonesia strengthened the hand of
the Army against the Communist Party in a struggle whose outcome has had the most profound international implications.

But the greater public also gets into the act in a more regular, generally more peaceable way, in the form of periodic elections in the democracies—and even some of the semidemocracies, if not the "guided" democracies. In such elections, international matters can, and often do, enter as central issues of the campaign. In these election situations, public opinion polling is, of course, playing an increasing role, not only in the United States but in many other countries.

World-Wide Consensuses

Having a while ago given half of the pollster's defense against Dean Acheson away by admitting that on a wide range of international issues the greater public does not have meaningful opinions, I must now take at least partial issue with his conclusion that "world opinion simply does not exist on matters that concern us." In general, this, no doubt, is correct; but in certain cases—admittedly rare—there *are* world-wide, or virtually world-wide, reactions or consensuses on matters that do concern us.

One that comes to mind has to do with the Suez affair in 1956. I have little doubt that the well-nigh universal condemnation of the Israeli-British-French invasion of Egypt in the United Nations was supported by what can only be called a consensus of world opinion—a consensus shared by many people in the United Kingdom and France.

Another is the world-wide impact of Russia's launching of the first two Sputniks in 1957, followed by its subsequent achievements in space. These developments led to re-evaluations of the relative standing of the two superpowers, extending not only through official circles and elites, but to general publics as well,[11] which helped to contribute, along with other developments, to the idea that a nuclear stalemate now exists—a notion which has affected the foreign policies of most of the nations of the world.

An example of a completely different sort was the universal reaction of horror and grief, among both high and low, set off by the assassination of President Kennedy. I would also maintain that there is a world-wide image of the United States, with many common elements, shared even by many illiterates.[12] In this connection, I would like to bring out a fact which may surprise most Americans and reassure what Dean Acheson calls their "Narcissus psychosis." The studies done by USIA, ourselves and others, show that the over-all image of the United States abroad is eminently favorable at the abstract level of opinions about America. In fact, taking the globe as a whole, the United States is unquestionably the most popular major power in the history of the world, despite the evidence of sporadic anti-American demonstrations and the burning of USIS libraries.

My final example is one of *potential* impact on what could only be called world opinion. I have no doubt that a truly world-wide reaction of great intensity would be kicked off against any power which first resorted to nuclear weapons anywhere in today's world.

Regional and National Consensuses

Short of these relatively rare global consensuses, there are certain basic attitudes so widely held in certain regions or areas of the world that they must be taken into account, both by the governments which rule there and by others dealing with them. The phobia in Latin America against "American intervention" is one example. Similarly, in almost all of Africa and Asia, basic attitude patterns opposed to "imperialism" and "colonialism" are deeply rooted. So, for example, is the anti-Israeli "set" of the Arab world; and, fortunately for us, the anti-Chinese bias in much of Southeast Asia.

In addition, there are many situations where there is a meaningful consensus of public opinion in particular countries, based upon common assumptions and attitudes in regard to certain issues the public has made matters of its own concern. One example is the widespread support for the United Nations by the public in the United States.[13] Another is the almost universal aspiration of West Germans for the reunification of Germany. At present, too, I cannot help but believe that, despite their "ignorance," most villagers in India have very intense opinions about Pakistan, no matter how uninformed they may be about the specifics of the Kashmir issue. Then there is the fear and hatred of the Germans among most Russians and Poles, not to mention the anti-German bias of the public in the United Kingdom. Another example is the general opposition of the Japanese public to the full-scale rearmament of Japan.

Domestic Opinion

The time has come to put this matter into some perspective. To start with, let us admit that, by and large, most of the time, public opinion, whether at home or abroad, has little relevance to the hundreds of day-to-day decisions on routine policy problems made by our Department of State and other foreign offices. Meaningful opinion on such specifics either does not exist, or, where it does exist, is usually so weak, either as to the proportion of the public holding a given view or as to the intensity of their feeling, that it has little significance. However, when it comes to the basics of a country's foreign policy and its international posture, government policy-makers themselves live in a certain climate of opinion. They are members of their own society and they share many, if not most, of the common assumptions—and hence attitudes—on fundamentals involved in whatever consensuses exist in that society, if only among its elite. Beyond this, when the polls show that the public supports a given policy, the decision-makers will usually be reassured and feel reinforced in their pursuance of that line of action.

On the other hand, in any particular country, there are programs and policies for which no leader, no matter how popular or expert, can engender popular endorsement. In other words, the climate of opinion imposes limits, sometimes very broad, sometimes very narrow, on each government's area of maneuver. In the extreme, certain things are virtually taboo; in other cases, they are merely impolitic; in others, anything is possible, particularly where public opinion is either nonexistent, weak, or divided.

Even totalitarian governments are subject to some restraints imposed by popular psychology. For example, the desire for a better standard of living among the Soviet people is now so strong that the last thing the leadership wants is another armaments race with the United States, which would divert more resources from butter to guns. This is almost certainly one of the reasons the Soviet government agreed to the nuclear test ban treaty, and why Soviet policy has been generally nonprovocative since the Cuban missile flare-up.

Needless to say, strong leaders sometimes fly squarely in the face of domestic opinion. For example, President de Gaulle is pursuing policies opposed to the integration of Western Europe despite the fact that the French Institute of Public Opinion's figures have consistently shown overwhelming support for "Europe" at the public level. According to most observers, however, De Gaulle has paid a price for this obduracy in the way of diminished popular support.

Foreign Opinion

Even more often, governments do and, indeed, must fly in the face of public opinion abroad. This is particularly true of the

United States as it plays its role of world leadership. In particular cases, this simply cannot be helped; everyone cannot be pleased. If we aid India to rearm against the Chinese threat, we are bound to incur the wrath of the Pakistanis. We cannot assist Israel without provoking an anti-American outburst from the Arab world, or vice versa. We cannot fight the war in Vietnam without enraging the "doves" in many parts of the world.

No responsible critic of current practices that I have ever come across has maintained that our government, or any government, should slavishly follow foreign public opinion; nor that our foreign policy should be based, exclusively or primarily, upon courting momentary popularity abroad. Our position is a much more modest one. It is that, for the United States to be maximally effective in its role of world leadership, public opinion and other psychological data should be cranked into the over-all intelligence appraisals of given situations; and that, at all levels of government, psychological factors should be taken into account, among other factors, in framing foreign policies and adopting and enunciating international positions.

You may well ask: "But isn't this so obviously desirable in today's world that it is already being done?" The answer is, not nearly enough; and, most emphatically, not *systematically* enough —even where public opinion data are available, which most of the time is not the case with the limited research efforts now being conducted.

The Research Potential

Much more could be said; but, with apologies to Dean Acheson, I believe the point has been made that there *are* widely shared attitudes on international matters, whether global, regional, or national, which governments simply must take into account and can ignore only at their peril. And the best way to find out about these with certainty and understanding, I would contend, is through public opinion research.

When it comes to such research, the sky is potentially the limit— or should I say the moon, once it has been colonized? Apart from political conditions which may make such an operation difficult or impossible, it is methodologically feasible by now, given the proper approach and facilities, to interview almost any type of people, anywhere on the earth today, from the most primitive to the most sophisticated. In addition to a number of international networks (of which the Gallup Poll and Elmo Wilson's International Research Associates are the leading examples), there are local research organizations, of varying degrees of competency, capable of carrying out opinion studies in many countries of the world today.[14] We pollsters even have our own international organization: WAPOR, the World Association of Public Opinion Research, with membership from more than forty countries.

The need, however, is not only for *more* psychological data but for *better* psychological data. For research utilizing public opinion techniques to develop its full potential, it should go into matters more basic than "attitudes" and "opinions." It should investigate "reality worlds" in general and the assumptions, often latent or implicit, upon which attitudes and opinions are founded. It should look into the aspirations, preoccupations, values, frustrations, and allegiances of the people studied. For deeper understanding, it should be carried forward on a trend basis to show changes systematically. For fuller meaningfulness, the findings should be interpreted against a broader background of social science data: studies of the power and influence structure in particular societies; of "national character," to use one of the older terms; of the "political culture," to refer to one of the newer concepts.[15]

Especially if this is done, it is my belief that public opinion research can make a vital contribution—far more than it is presently contributing—not only toward the more effective conduct of foreign relations by our own and other governments, but toward our broadest international goal: a more stable, viable, happy, democratically oriented world, with greater mutual understanding between peoples, if not peace.

5

PROBLEM SOLVING:
THE BEHAVIORAL APPROACH

Karl Deutsch
Harvard University

I should like to discuss problem-solving in international relations and the contributions of the behavioral science approach.

In political analysis the first task is to form some sort of reasonably coherent idea of the *context* of international politics. The second is to *define* the problem. It makes a great difference whether we define an international confrontation as a conflict of good versus evil, or as a failure in communication between two countries. It makes a very great difference whether we think that the essential problem is achieving a balance of power, adjustment to secular change, or a decision-maker's ignorance of technological change.

Third, we must try to discover the *preferences* of the decision-makers on both sides and the *costs* of alternative policies. This opens up the possibility of a cost-benefit analysis, which may enable us to tell the decision-maker not what his preferences ought to be, but what price tags should be attached to his preferences and policies.

Up to this point the social scientist is the servant of the decision-maker. He says, if this is what you want to do, these are the cheapest ways of doing it, and even if you take the cheapest or the most efficient way (and there are two or three alternative ways you might choose), these are the costs in each case: the costs in time, in wealth, possibly in danger, and in human suffering.

I submit, however, that the social scientist has one more duty. His fourth task is to use his cognitive and critical powers to reveal the *normative implications* of each policy choice which the decision-maker faces. He has to ask whether the preferences which he discerns in the "utility schedule," the preference schedule of the decision-maker, are in fact compatible with each other. Although human beings invented logic, they are often illogical, which makes them perhaps more endearing. But the result is that not only high officials and middle-range executives, but also the average voter in many countries (or the average party activist in totalitarian countries), frequently entertains several preferences which may not be consistent with each other. It therefore becomes the difficult and potentially dangerous duty of the social scientist to point out that two policies cannot, in fact, be pursued simultaneously. Or he may have to point out that one value, if pursued, particularly if pursued beyond a certain moderate range, entails a loss of another value.

Here the approach of the social scientist becomes inevitably tinged with a normative concern, for he cannot avoid dealing with the problem of legitimacy. In searching for a repeatable, describable test of legitimacy, we might say that it is legitimate to pursue one value in such a way, or within such limits, as not to inflict intolerable damage on another value by the same decision-maker. It is legitimate for a man to spend money to improve his health, but not to the point of ruining himself and his family. It is legitimate for a man to spend some of his energy in earning an income, provided that in the process he does not destroy his health and that of his family. You all know the old joke about the businessman who said that he first ruined his health to make money and now was losing his money trying to regain his health. These are simple examples from everyday life, but, at bottom, the concept of legitimacy implies that we cannot pursue one value too far without destroying some other value, or damaging it to an intolerable degree. This is based on a proposition which I think can be verified from a good deal of evidence we have about human behavior: men do not live by bread alone, nor do they live by any one value alone. Human beings are essentially and inevitably beings steered by a plurality of values, all of which are essential to their functioning. Legitimacy, then, is the set of rules or propositions governing the consistency or compatibility of these essential values at a particular time and place.

When the social scientist presents evidence as to what the effects of the pursuit of one value will be upon another value, he is speaking about legitimacy, and it is important for him to consult the philosopher of politics, the philosopher of law, the leader, in terms that are relevant to their concerns. The normative approach to political behavior, national and international, is an essential part of our relevant universe of discourse. No sharp line separates social science from normative concerns. On the contrary, the normative concern about the legitimacy and compatibility of values is an essential concern of the social scientist. And the social scientist's evidence is of essential concern to the normative philosopher. We are dealing here with different aspects of what is in essence one indivisible dialogue.

The fifth and last task is that of *developing the mind* of the decision-maker—the person who must make a judgment for scholarship, for history, or for practical action on an international relations problem. We try to find out how to get hard data; we try to discover patterns and models and configurations which help us to judge. But in another less tangible, but no less real way, we are developing the minds of people. We are trying to develop our own judgment, including our emotions and our intuitions, and the judgments, the emotions, and the intuitions of our students.

This is analogous to the problem of clinical judgment in the field of medicine. A medical doctor must learn many facts—hard data on the amount of blood-sugar a person must have in his blood, or the amount of strychnine a guinea pig can tolerate. He must learn many specific and very precise techniques. He must learn many models and patterns, such as the concept of the circulation of the blood, the germ theory of disease, and the concept of vitamin deficiency diseases. (Every one of those I have named began life as a scientific theory.) But on top of all this a good doctor must actually have seen a large number of sick people. From his experience with many patients he develops a special kind of judgment. He develops what is sometimes called a "mellow"—more sensitive, more perceptive—mind, which is as essential to the making of a good doctor as are blood counts, X-ray pictures, electrocardiograms, and medical statistics. The doctor whose patients have a better chance of survival is one whose training includes hard data and precise techniques, and whose experience has given him depth, richness, and humanity of judgment.

Perception of the Context of International Relations

Let me give you some examples of the types of analysis I have been referring to. Our first and most fundamental question was:

what kind of a world is it in which an international relations problem has to be judged? Does the evidence tell us that most nations and most individuals are motivated by self-interest? Is it an interest that has important ideological, religious, and other components as stated in the more traditional, descriptive, but often deeply perceptive literature, such as the analyses by Hans Morgenthau or George Kennan? Is it on the whole realistic even to assume that decision-makers know their own interests?

Is international relations a world of all against all, as envisaged by Thomas Hobbes? Can peace be established only by some supersovereign in the Hobbesian style? Or is international relations a marvelous Adam Smithian universe where an invisible hand restores again and again the balance of power so that large countries and small can preserve the European concert for uncounted centuries in a minuet of ever changing coalitions? Is the international society a Manichean universe where the forces of dark and light, of evil and good are eternally contending? Or is it a Manichean world at the verge of salvation, so that one more war to end war, one more crusade to make the world safe for democracy, one more "*lutte finale*" for the Communist utopia will suddenly change and transform the world once for all into something radically better?

Or is international politics best described as the professional nightmare of the safety or collision engineer? Are the ships of state going at full speed through the fog like the *Titanic*—described as unsinkable by its designers—with little attention being paid to the falling thermometer on the bridge, and the icebergs waiting out ahead in the fog? Such a vision was described by Søren Kierkegaard in 1840 and enacted by the *Titanic* in 1912. Or may we compare international politics with the ships *Stockholm* and *Andrea Doria*, running through fog, each captain sure he is on the correct course, and after the collision asserting that it was the other's fault?

We are dealing with a world containing over 100 states, each of which is struggling to adjust to a fantastically accelerating pace of change—economic, sociological, technological, and psychological. Are the governments in danger of losing control? Are they afraid of losing control of the processes of change in their own countries, and thus finding it even harder to control their relations with other countries? This is a problem of adjustment, the kind which the international relations literature describes as the "problem of peaceful change."

Let me raise a second question. Just as our perception of a problem depends upon our notion of what the international system is like, it also depends critically upon our notion of what human beings are like. We have for a long time been familiar with various statements about human nature which according to the odd-numbered writers cannot be changed, and according to the even-numbered writers is changing. But we have not spent very much time and attention on finding out what repeated observations are telling us about human nature under different circumstances and in different places. In the last thirty years, a vast literature on the nature of human behavior has become available for the first time; it tells us in considerably more detail, and with considerably more precision and reliability, what human beings are really like.

How do human beings react when frightened? Do they become more rational or less? The theory of deterrence depends critically upon the rationality of a government that has just been threatened very seriously and credibly with nuclear destruction. We ought to know something about what psychologists have found out about the precision of the rational processes of badly frightened men. We know something about whether rationality increases or deteriorates under stress. We have a great deal of material about stress. But I know of no book on deterrence that pays any attention to the findings of psychologists about rationality under prolonged stress, or about rationality under prolonged and serious frustration. We have by now large compendia of potentially relevant data. We have an inventory by Berelson and Steiner which lists about a thousand reasonably verified propositions on how human beings behave. We have two volumes by Otto Klineberg, summarizing a good deal of the psychological literature, *Tensions Affecting International Understanding* and a later volume on *The Human Dimension in International Relations*. We can now begin to ask questions much more systematically. What are human beings like as individuals? What are they like in small groups? How do they behave as organized governments or nations? Can foreigners be intimidated by tactics which we are intuitively sure would not intimidate Americans but merely provoke them? Are foreigners as different from us as all that? If so, when and where? If not, what would be the implications of our use of threats? If somebody wanted to get the United States to the negotiating table, would bombing any part of our territory make us more likely to enter negotiations? If not, why do we assume that the people or government of North Vietnam can be made to negotiate by bombing them? Do we have profound experts on North Vietnamese psychology who have made these decisions? If so, who are they?

We are interested in discovering when and how other people react as we react, and when they will react differently. We know in general the effects of bombing on morale. We have massive and impressive strategic bombing surveys, made for the United States Air Force by expert psychologists in Germany and in Japan after World War II. I remember a figure from one of them which indicated that in German cities that had undergone heavy bombardment morale was slightly higher than in German cities which had not been bombed.

We may try to familiarize ourselves with the concept of systems and system levels. In very many ways the decision system of a single individual can be thought of as a little society of memories, preferences, and desires. This idea is at least as old as Plato's *Republic*. We can think of a group as making up its mind—a small group is often treated as if it were a person. We can personify nations. We can say that in certain important ways the pattern of communications within an individual, within a group, and within a nation have striking and important analogies. It is fruitful to follow these analogies. But we can also remember that it is quite possible for a system to have properties which are radically different from its components. Every day at five o'clock in the afternoon, in many cities in the United States, insane traffic patterns are created by perfectly sane motorists who quite reasonably want nothing else but to get home quickly. Yet the traffic pattern produces a tie-up which forces them to move slowly, if at all.

In 1914 the governments of Europe, even the German government, thought of themselves as reasonably cautious and not given to panic. Yet in the existing system of European politics and strategic decision-making, every army had to be prepared for instant mobilization, and the first state to mobilize would, other things being equal, have the advantage on the battlefield. When war threatened, this system produced a result comparable to the panic at the Coconut Grove fire, when men and women trampled one another in a mad dash for the exits. In 1914 relatively rational governments had made themselves part of a radically irrational system. As Winston Churchill afterward summed it up: "A situation had been created in which statesmen had only to do their duty to wreck the world. They did their duty."

Perception of Specific Problems

Within this framework, what kind of problems would be worth investigating? Let us remember that the practical statesman first has to deal with a specific problem, and becomes aware of its broader context only as he proceeds to analyze it. Was the anti-colonial movement in Tanganyika in 1957, for example, a genuine movement for self-government? Or was it an artificially stirred-up agitation with nobody behind it but a handful of malcontents? The governor of Tanganyika in 1957 thought it was the latter. It turned out that he was wrong. It would have been possible, by the methods of behavioral science, to find out how large a proportion of the population in Tanganyika had entered life situations in which they were likely to become interested in politics. It would have been possible to find out how many people were active in public affairs, how many people were going to be willing to vote, or to pay money, or to go on strike, or to demonstrate, and therefore to some extent to find out how large the support for Nyerere and his movement was going to be by 1959, or by 1960.

Is a government *de facto* strong or stable or popular, or is it not? For example, does General de Gaulle represent basic views and aspirations of many Frenchmen? Or are his policies merely idio-syncrasies of a strong and self-willed old war hero which will be dropped as soon as he retires from the active leadership of French affairs? This is an important problem and we could get evidence on it one way or the other. Does M. Lecanuet, with his more pro-American policies, represent the majority consensus of the French people? Or does he represent no more than a respectable and impressive 16 per cent—or, according to other data, 9 per cent—of the French voters? Are the old political parties in France dead? Or is there a survival of French parties? A survey in March 1964 told us that 70 per cent of French leaders were quite sure that the politi-cal parties were not dead. The elections of March 1965, a year later, confirmed this, and so did the first round of the French presidential elections of December 1966.

Is a government in a foreign country a foreign puppet, or is it genuine? For instance, was the Chinese Communist government of 1951 a Russian puppet, or was it genuinely Chinese? Dean Rusk was quoted in 1951 as denying that Mr. Mao's government was Chinese. A great deal hinged on a decision of that sort, and a good deal of evidence could have been found about it, one way or the other. Are Communist governments part of a single, worldwide conspiracy, or are they divided into sovereign states with distinct national interests? How soon could one find how much evidence there is on either side of this proposition? Is the Soviet bloc likely to integrate more firmly into a single Communist world, or is it disintegrating? Is the integration of Western Europe progressing steadily, accelerating, or slowing down? When and how do its trends change? Has it stopped? When? How? Why? In countries plagued by subversion, is the recruitment rate of the guerrilla movement larger or smaller than their attrition rate? Are the government troops losing more soldiers than they are taking in? What were the initial levels of the forces on each side? What are their rates of growth and decline? What is likely to be their future, if left to themselves; what external reinforcements will be needed in order to keep one or the other side still active in the field? Is a particular confrontation a game of bluff between two governments, a chain of escalation, or a failure of communication?

We can look at such possibilities and then ask, still formulating the problem, what costs and what benefits do we wish to take into account in deciding, for example, whether or not to drop a nuclear weapon on the city of Hiroshima. Should we only take into account by how many days the Japanese surrender might be hastened? Professor Edwin O. Reischauer, formerly United States ambassador to Japan, states in his book *The United States and Japan* that the nuclear bomb at most hastened the Japanese surrender by only a few days. Should we also take into account the number of days, months, or years by which our demonstrating the

terrible power of the bomb would accelerate Joseph Stalin's nuclear weapons program? You may remember that Stalin, for ideological reasons, had a low opinion of the supposedly decadent
idealistic plutocratic physics of the Western world. The demonstration of Hiroshima was the most impressive evidence to make
Stalin allocate the scarcest and most valuable manpower and engineering resources of the Soviet Union to an accelerated nuclear
weapons program. What were the costs and benefits on one side?
What were they on the other? I am not talking about the intangible
or ethical costs and benefits. But even in the most cold-blooded
calculations of power politics, very much depends on how compre-
hensively and realistically the program is formulated. What proba-
bilities of proliferation are involved in a particular nuclear weapons
policy or a particular employment of airpower?

The Resources of Behavioral Science

I have given you examples of problems. Let me ask now, how,
if at all, can behavioral science help in dealing with such problems?
What is it anyway? I should propose two definitions for behavioral
science. One, behavioral science is any study of human behavior
which deals in impersonally reproducible evidence. Anything that
can be recorded or inferred by more than one observer from
impersonally observable actions is behavioral science. The statement of a poet about the condition of his soul may be evidence
about his state of mind. It is not a scientific statement. A nonrepro-
ducible and unrepeatable observation which is not based on traces
which can be observed repeatedly by others may be very important
but it is not scientific. If more than one person can repeat the
operation, then it may be called scientific. Behavioral science
depends on operations that can be accurately described, and that
can be repeated by more than one experimenter, observer, or
analyst. A second and somewhat broader definition considers

behavioral science any study which yields evidence that can be tested and compared with evidence from other independent operations.

Behavioral science is also a name for a collection of disciplines. When the Ford Foundation in the early fifties wanted to put up money for the study of the social sciences it was felt that some of its businessmen trustees might object to the term "social science" because it might remind them of socialism. Therefore, some of the psychologists proceeded to invent a term they hoped would be completely devoid of any emotional connotations. They coined the term "behavioral science" and the Ford Foundation called the grant "The Grant in the Behavioral Sciences." The term has since then acquired plenty of emotional connotations. However, it still refers to a collection of such disciplines as economics, sociology, psychology, psychiatry, anthropology, and political science, together with important aspects of history and that part of the study of literature which yields reproducible evidence.

These academic disciplines share the same problems, but they differ in that each discipline is based on distinct bodies of tradition, distinct standards of evaluation, distinct departments, budgets, journals, and bodies of expert referees for evaluation of work. The problems, however, are to a significant extent common. Indeed, the fact that each discipline has a separate pool of resources (and that is what a discipline is) has led the disciplines to exaggerate the distinctiveness of the problems with which they deal. For instance, economists for a long time have disdained to pay any attention to the psychology of consumers. Finally, Professor James Duesenberry took his place on the Council of Economic Advisors. An economist with psychological interests was given the accolade. But for quite a long time psychological evidence was somehow considered outside the realm of economics. And of course the psychologists were not expected to know economics.

The techniques, again, are overlapping. The different bodies of resources that we call economic disciplines all have been hit in the last thirty years by the discovery of new techniques. Perhaps the most fundamental and far-reaching (and you may well differ with my judgment in this) is the discovery of statistical sampling. It has been found that we can very often make worthwhile statements about large bodies of facts or cases by examining only a small portion, if this portion has been selected in accordance with certain rules given in the science of probability. How to pick a good sample is a problem of science. But with a good sample it is possible, by interviewing 3,000 American voters, to forecast an American election—usually within 4 per cent of accuracy. By now, forecasting has become standard in most countries. You can do much the same for the sale of toothpaste or of other commodities. The one area in which pretesting by sampling methods has not been much used is foreign policy. But science can tell you how to use samples; and with this has come a shift of our viewpoints from determinism to probability, and a shift from descriptive literature to interviews. For we are beginning much more to consult the people about whose attitudes we theorize. We are trying to behave less like veterinarians and more like doctors; we are talking to our patients.

The interview method has taken the social scientist out of his study and out of the library into the field. If he is a good social scientist he comes back to the library and compares his findings with what other people have found. But it does mean he has to move around. We are moving around more these days in our profession than we used to and that is probably inevitable. The anthropologists have to look at Indians, and the students of foreign relations have to talk to foreigners. There is no way around it.

We are now doing survey research both on the mass level and on the elite opinion level. One technique consists of asking many people a few questions (this is the opinion poll type), and another is the depth interview that asks a great many questions of a few people. You can have a depth interview that runs from $1\frac{1}{2}$ to 2 hours or, as Robert Lane's work has shown, it can run up to 14 hours and continue for two or three consecutive sessions, recording on tape all of the subject's replies, followed by the analysis of this material for months afterward. We have projective tests in which people are asked to say what they think of in response to certain stimuli, such as the ambiguous pictures of the Thematic Apperception Test. By these means we can find out the variations in attitudes among South Italian peasants, North Italian factory workers, and Kansas farmers toward such topics as industry, thrift, and the future. This was done with fascinating results by Edward Banfield.

We can use content analysis, either by hand, so to speak—setting up a number of categories and having the analyst do the best he can to judge the replies—or we can do this now by machine. It is possible to set up a dictionary: we embody our questions and theories in a dictionary in which we say, "the following 100 words all connote hostility and the following names are the people we are interested in." We then put a text of, let us say, a sample of editorials from the newspaper onto punched cards and run them through a high speed computer, instructing it to make a note whenever, let us say, the United States is mentioned, when the United States is mentioned in a context of hostility, how often in a context that is friendly or favorable, and how often in a context that seems to be neither as far as the computer is concerned. The computer could then trace quite nicely whether the friendliness of a newspaper to the United States is increasing or declining, and if the sample is well chosen, the computer's judgment will stand up. It will be reproducible. If you take a second or a third sample, or split your sample in half and do the analysis twice, you can have somewhat more confidence in the result. By the way, in the days when I taught at the Fletcher School, some of these researches were still being made by graduate students; it will please them to know that this particular job is something which no longer has to be done by human labor. The scholar can now do this efficiently by giving the task to the machine and spending his time devising a more ingenious questionnaire or dictionary of content analysis. The anthropologists have developed a technique for searching out "themes" in a culture, in its artifacts, its stories, its communications, and in the protocols of their informants. From all this we can build up a very considerable amount of evidence about the attitudes and images which people have about matters which are relevant to foreign policy problems.

We can test all this against aggregate data, that is, against the data that tell us how people actually behave. Two countries say that they like each other very much. Very well. Do they trade with each other? Do they trade with each other about as much as corresponds to their total share in world trade, neither more nor less? Do they trade much more? Or much less? If we program a computer to test all the different flows of commodity trade in the world, let us say between 106 countries, with the resulting matrix of roughly 10,000 trade relations, the computer will pick out the colonial empires, if you use the data for 1938. The computer has never heard of empires, but they will come out quite clearly, and it turns out that Grover Clark's book on *The Balance Sheets of Imperialism* was statistically naive. We have found out that political relationships do make a major difference, that trade indeed does, to some degree, follow the flag, once you correct for the size of the countries participating in the process.

We can then find out whether this relation increases or decreases, whether pairs of countries are getting closer together or farther apart. And what we can do for trade we can also do for travel, for the exchange of students, and for a good many other international transactions. We can then compare attitudes with actual behavior.

The evidence should tell us what the effects of attitudes are on actions. We know that from surveys on voting intentions we can predict the results of an election within a relatively modest range of error. We would be happy indeed in international politics if our error range were not greater than 4 per cent in most cases. We can, conversely, find out what happens when an event impinges on a set of attitudes, that is, what change in attitudes or images is produced by external events. A study of international political behavior edited by Herbert Kelman has evidence on these points. It turns out that it takes a fairly drastic event to shift between 10 and 20 per cent of the voters. A shift of 30 to 40 per cent requires a really tremendous international event which is fully reported by the national mass media and emphasized by actions of the government. That is to say, it turns out that mass opinion is on the whole less volatile and more stable, statistically, than one would have thought. But again, in very many policy situations a shift of 10 or 20 per cent of the voters can make a very large difference and it is good to know what the size of the change could be.

Finally, behavioral science has given us the perception of new patterns. For example, through game theory, it has marked the distinctions between so-called "fight patterns" (I am here quoting Professor Anatol Rapoport), that is, patterns of escalation which work like processes of nature. Each protagonist takes as his starting point the behavior of his opponent. A dog sees another dog and growls. The other dog growls back, the first dog's hackles rise, the second dog's hackles rise, now teeth are bared, a snarl follows, then a snap, a bite, and a dog fight. One great nation confronts another great nation, aspersions are cast, insults are exchanged, border incidents follow, and in a short time you may have an Indian-Pakistani war or an Arab-Israeli escalation. That is to say, these are in important respects quasi-automatic fight processes, or escalation processes, and these, such as arms races, can be described by pairs of differential equations. It is a good thing to know by now what these processes are, to know the sequences, to know how they work, to know what to expect if such a sequence of events is not interrupted or broken up quickly.

We know on the other hand that there is an entirely different kind of international situation: the game. In a game, players have a rational choice between alternative strategies. The outcome of each strategy, however, does not depend only on the desire of the player, but depends critically on what the other player will do, which cannot be controlled. In a game, the rational choices for decisions are variable. It is given that each player desires to win. In other words, in a game situation the values of the two players are irrevocably fixed.

The third type of confrontation is debate. In a serious debate, the factual perceptions, and perhaps even some of the preferences of the partners in the debate, are susceptible to variation. What you hear may help you to change your mind. In this sense, college debating is a very unfortunate exercise because the debate is only a game. The debating team is supposed to win. In law, also, the defense lawyer is supposed to put the best case for his client, rather than conceding the argument to the prosecutor.

We have separated the function of the judge and that of the advocate in adversary proceedings. But in many social situations, and in many international situations, we are not merely lawyers; we are also judges—at least judges of our own interests. If today we would be the lawyers only for the interests we conceived of yesterday, we would lose our chance for a fresh judgment of our own interests. And yet so much of international politics is cast in the role of the fight, or at best, in the role of the game. You might say that Thomas Schelling and others deserve our gratitude in having elevated our image of foreign policy from the level of the dog fight to the level of the game. This is a great piece of intellectual progress, and potentially of moral progress, too.

Our next step would be to see to what extent we can regain what the game player has lost: the judgment of his own range of preferences and long-range interests. A particular example of this is the famous prisoner's dilemma game. According to the classical anecdote, two prisoners in an Oriental city were brought before the governor of the town, who told them, "You are both suspected of a crime. We don't have enough evidence to convict either of you, and we can convict you only on evidence, so a confession is essential." He saw each of these prisoners separately. "If you," he told the first of the two wretches, "will confess, you will be let free with a sum of money. Of course your partner, the other fellow, will be hanged, but that's not your problem." "Well, your excellency," said the prisoner, "what happens if the other fellow confesses first?" "Oh, then you will be hanged and he gets the money." "Well, your excellency, excuse me if I keep asking questions, but what happens if neither of us confesses?" "Well, then, you will both be let free, but you won't get any money." "And what happens if we both confess at about the same time?" "Oh, well, then you each get twenty years in prison. Now go back to your cell and think it over." The prisoner went back, consulted his standard handbook on Game Theory (Von Neumann and Morgenstern) and made the most rational decision he could. This decision was that obviously he could not trust that crook, the other fellow. Since it was likely the other fellow would cheat, he had better confess first. The other fellow, of course, figured that he could not trust the first, and hence he had to confess first. They both rang the bell, called the keeper, and both rushed to the Governor, confessed, and then had twenty years in jail to think about their rationality.

This story of two prisoners in an Oriental jail parallels the story of two countries which do not know whether to keep an arms control agreement, or whether to cheat on a nuclear test ban; and there are dozens of other examples of this. We now have evidence of a hundred thousand plays where "prisoners' dilemma" games were played by teams of people under laboratory conditions, and a large amount of evidence is becoming available about what people do in actual experience.

Let me give you two bits of information, just to tell you what one can learn about prisoners' dilemma games. One, people begin typically to play such games with roughly 50 per cent cooperative behavior; that is, each refuses to sell out the other fellow. But during the first fifty repetitions they become disappointed when they fail to coordinate their moves, and each finds himself double-crossed by the other. After about fifty plays, cooperation is reduced to one-quarter of the cases. They have acquired the cynicism of the newly initiated. Then after about another fifty games down in the trough of mutual noncooperativeness, they gradually signal to each other and work themselves up. For the last fifty or a hundred plays of a three-hundred-play run, they level out at about 73 to 75 per cent cooperative behavior.

The average of men over the whole three hundred plays therefore works out at about 53 per cent cooperative, but the end stages are about 73 per cent cooperative. Teams of women playing against each other show only half as much cooperation. (This should be borne in mind before you take a teaching job at a women's college.) The men-women teams are between the two, but the men seem to pull twice as much; that is, they are only one-third away from the male average and two-thirds away from the female average.

There is a more interesting point. When the matrix of the payoffs for each possible outcome of the prisoners' dilemma game is visibly displayed in front of the players at all times, the frequency of cooperative behavior doubles. It seems that the philosopher Immanuel Kant was right. Consciousness does help moral behavior. If people know what the situation is, they can adjust to a relatively higher systems level than if they have only to trust their memories of it.

I will not take the time to give you a set of examples for another concept—the social mobilization process—which also can be linked to experimental evidence, and which shows how all over the world more and more people are moving from rural isolation into cities, from subsistence economy to freer use of money, and from political apathy to potential and later actual interest in politics. I would like to cite two figures, though, in this connection. In 1830, 30,000 Frenchmen conquered Algeria. In 1960, 600,000 Frenchmen could not hold it. In the Congo in 1959 and 1960, one armed man could keep peace of a sort among 500 civilians. In Algeria in 1960 one armed man could not keep peace among fifteen Algerian Muslims. That is, the police ratio has changed from about one in 500 to one in fifteen. I have taken two extreme cases to show what the size of the social mobilization process can be.

We are facing all over the world increasingly literate, increasingly money-using, increasingly urban, and increasingly unruly populations. All countries are getting harder and harder to govern. The vision of George Orwell in his book *1984*—that modern technology would make government and supervision easier—was based on a pathetic ignorance of communication. It turns out that the factors in modernization that make governing more difficult are more powerful and faster than the increases in the hardware of supervision and repression, such as fingerprint equipment, television cameras, and "big brother" microphones under the bed. One of the reasons for this, of course, is that you can mechanize loudspeakers but you cannot mechanize listening. The total supervision of populations is therefore impractical.

In short, countries are getting harder to govern by their own nationals, and much harder to govern by foreigners. We might speak of a secular tendency toward a rising cost of foreign intervention. We can find this out by using as much evidence as we can. Or we can find it out the hard way by losing blood and treasure in trying to govern increasingly unmanageable foreign populations.

I would like to note briefly some examples of where the behavioral sciences have been applied to specific cases and of where they could have been applied and were not. In international affairs, one of the first major attempts to get behavioral science evidence was made in the Second World War by the United States on its own soldiers' morale, in the famous studies by Paul Lazarsfeld, Samuel Stouffer, and others. Studies on enemy morale were conducted by Edward Shils and Morris Janowitz on German prisoners of war as to why they did or did not surrender. This study is still a classic in the field. Similar studies were made by Alexander Leighton on Japanese surrenders in World War II.

In addition to this we had the studies by Ruth Benedict, Alexander Leighton, and others on Japanese national character. The study by Rear Admiral Ellis Zacharias on how many ships the Japanese had lost, and Ambassador Grew's political and descriptive judgment, converged in the finding that Japan was likely to surrender in the summer of 1945 or before the end of 1945. If the situation had occurred twenty years later, the margin of uncertainty that came out of these four studies could have been reduced. The amount of their convergence could have been greater. Nevertheless, a decisive insight, namely that Japanese surrender was going to be greatly facilitated by giving Japan at least informal assurances that the Imperial system would be retained, seems to have come not only out of the judgment of Ambassador Grew and the diplomats, but also out of the independent evidence of the anthropologists and the data which they had examined.

Let me give as another example a study on western European integration which was carried on at Yale. We found from aggregate data that, on the whole, the trade integration of western Europe halted so far as structural integration is concerned about 1957; from then on what increases there were in intra-European trade among the Six could be accounted for by the sheer effects of prosperity rather than by any further structural change. We found the same in other fields of transactions in addition to commodity trade. We found that France's secession from the consensus on Western foreign policy began in 1955. On the mass opinion level the French began to move away from American, British, German, and Italian views, and stayed away thereafter. These converging streams of evidence tell us something about what can and what cannot be done about western European integration here and now, but also what possibilities and opportunities remain open for the future.

The same group of studies also revealed that the supposedly strong West German demand for national nuclear weapons, or for national access to such weapons, was to a large extent a myth; hence there was no strong political need to appease such a demand by creating a multilateral nuclear force (MLF) in which the German Federal Republic and its military personnel would move a great deal closer to the control of nuclear weapons. Our data, collected from interviews held in the summer of 1964, showed that there were minority groups in Germany who perhaps wanted nuclear weapons, but that they could not carry a German election. We forecast that it would not be practical for any party to get any mileage out of the nuclear weapons issue in the 1965 elections. It turned out that nobody did, and that the attempts of former Defense Minister Franz Joseph Strauss to make an issue out of the demand for nuclear weapons had no echo.

Let me give examples where behavioral research was not applied. The partition of India and Pakistan in 1947 was such a case. It would have been quite easy to forecast that India and Pakistan

could not form one political community, and that Moslem minorities in Hindu cities and Hindu minorities in Moslem cities in many
cases were in danger. It was possible to find out in advance that
this was particularly the case where the minority was a group of
moneylenders, landlords, or those in some other unpopular occupation. If this had been foreseen, the British could have evacuated
the endangered minorities before leaving India, and one million
lives could have been saved.

On a smaller scale, it would have been possible by behavioral
science methods to find out how well Greeks and Turks were
likely to get along in Cyprus. There a number of lives could have
been saved by timely evacuation and disentanglement; relocation
or resettlement in Cyprus would of course have only gone into
the hundreds, but these lives would have been saved.

The third example: I had the pleasure of welcoming in my seminar Sir Henry Willink, the Chairman of the Commission who
wrote the now defunct Constitution of Nigeria. He was asked,
"Why had the Constitution been so drawn as to give to the North,
the most backward and illiterate part of Nigeria, the greatest
amount of power and control?" He answered that it had been done
because the North was conservative and it was desired to give more
power to conservatism. And secondly, he said half jokingly, the
North was dry and flat and its aristocratic elite could ride ponies
and play polo, and these polo players were found far more con-
genial by the foreign service personnel. Sir Henry had a sense of
humor. But by the time the dead body of the Prime Minister of
Nigeria was found by the roadside, and when this was followed
later by the killing of thousands of Ibos by Northerners, and this
followed by new violence, the original constitutional arrangement
looked less funny. A serious effort to find out who had the
capabilities, who was likely to accept what, where education was
centered, where the officers came from and who their relatives

were, could have, quite conceivably, given Nigeria a better chance to shape its political fate with less bloodshed, even if perhaps as a loose federation, or even as a group of countries rather than as a single one.

A scientific decision, like a medical decision, is object-oriented. The goal is to find out what is true. A political decision unfortunately is not object-oriented. I will never forget what Secretary of State Dean Rusk told the American Political Science Association in September 1965. He said that when we do anything in foreign policy we have at least thirty reasons for doing it. He said in effect, "when I then have to justify what we are doing to an audience, I try to decide which of the thirty reasons will communicate with this particular audience." This sounds on the one hand as if all decisions were supremely wise, because how could a decision not be wise if it is made for thirty reasons? And presumably for thirty good reasons, at that. But it does not mean, if you analyze it more carefully, that the political decision is oriented to the single central object of the decision, that what is supposed to be true is actually true, or that the policy supposed to work will work. Rather, among its thirty reasons, the decision is also oriented to the decision-maker's domestic political environment, to his mass popularity, to his influential supporters, and to his own self-image. In 1919, when Woodrow Wilson decided to campaign in a certain way for American entry into the League of Nations he was not only oriented to get the United States into the League; he was at least as much oriented to defending his own image as a righteous man, and to establishing the image of his senatorial opponents as men of iniquity. He succeeded, at least in his own eyes, in the second object, even though he lost on the first.

Finally, there is the question of whether a certain policy will be accepted by the validators of a leader—the voters, Congress, important interest groups, and the press. The net result is that if you have to think of so many things to make a decision work, the primary objective—the pragmatic success of the decision in the foreign field—becomes a secondary question. If a doctor would most of the time try to decide, not whether the patient's appendix is inflamed or not, and whether it can or cannot be taken out, but whether this would please the relatives of the patient, and what it would do to the doctor's golf schedule, and the emotional climate in the community, and relations with the hospital, then the undertakers would be busier than they are. The doctors have learned to put the welfare of the patient first. And we may have to learn to establish a certain discontinuity between domestic and foreign politics.

As an issue of domestic politics we may decide to put a federal training school into a certain community, not because it is the best place to have it but because we need the local senator's vote for something else, and because the location is not obviously and critically worse. We make political decisions based on multiple orientations, where their objective feasibility is only one consideration and often not a critical one. In decisions about war and peace, in decisions about the life and death of individuals, of whole countries, and perhaps of mankind, this plural orientation is not good enough. I think the practitioners of international analysis, whether in public service or in academic world, must learn what the practitioners of medicine have learned. When it comes to a decision about war and peace there should be only two considerations: the truth of the situation and the survival of human beings.

6

THE IMPORTANCE
OF NATIONAL CULTURES

Margaret Mead
American Museum of Natural History

I am sometimes introduced to audiences as a pioneer in the application of cultural anthropology to the conduct of international affairs. I did, indeed, participate in the applications made of this science during World War II, and worked with other anthropologists to erect the first framework for a relationship between our scientific discipline and the world of international affairs.[1] As pioneers, we were able to build only a sort of log cabin, and unfortunately, a more ambitious structure has not been built to replace it. The early 1950's witnessed the petering out of research activities and applications held over from the war, and there have been practically no advances since. For examples of successes or failures, therefore, I must turn back to a period twenty years ago. Seen within the accelerated pace of today, the events of two decades ago seem like ancient history. They would hardly be worth recapitulating, if it were not for the fact that there is again some slight stirring of interest, both from students of international affairs and from anthropologists, in the contributions that can come from a knowledge of national culture and national character.

When World War II broke out, anthropologists realized that we were home for the duration. There would be no more field trips to the mountains of New Guinea, or to the jungles of South America, until the war was won. Furthermore, unlike the minor wars which followed it, World War II was a war to which we could wholeheartedly commit all our resources. I think it is always worth while to remind the present university generation of this fact. So complete was our commitment that, of the 300 anthropologists in the country, all but a half dozen were involved in some aspect of the war effort.

The summer before Pearl Harbor, a few of us had already begun to work on ways of securing a deeper understanding of Germany and Japan.[2] As soon as this country was involved in the war, many other anthropologists began looking for ways to contribute to the conduct of the war. The initiative was our own; we asked ourselves, as a profession that had no previous involvement in national problems, what we could do—and we started to organize ourselves so that we could do it. This meant the preparation of proposals, and the inauguration of preliminary explorations as small-scale researches. As these were introduced to the government, more and more social scientists were incorporated into the mushrooming federal apparatus. In this setting they had to deal with problems of morale, propaganda, psychological warfare, civilian defense, estimation of enemy and Allied capabilities and intentions, and the training of men for overseas assignments in contrasting cultures. Before World War II anthropologists had had very little contact with modern affairs. To be sure, they were occasionally consulted by governments. We were asked how to eliminate head-hunting without destroying a whole culture, or how to induce a people to accept some different and more hygienic form of burial. Very occasionally, we were asked how a group of American Indians living on reservations could be helped to establish a viable form of self-government. Until World War II, anthropology was concerned primarily with describing the cultures of primitive peoples. Because of the simplicity attendant on the lack of a script, primitive peoples provided a rare opportunity to study whole societies. Moreover, they were important to study because their way of life was disappearing under the impact of civilization. Whether using small societies as laboratories or acting as historians of vanishing cultures, anthropologists practiced what is today called *salvage* anthropology.

Our methods of research were adapted to the situations within which we worked. Sometimes, when we dealt with peoples who had a long history of contact, or when we sought to draw comparisons from the work of other anthropologists, we worked with library materials. But mainly we studied living people in living communities. Our data had to be elicited from the lips of the living. Characteristically, we worked in small communities, where all of the individuals could be known, and where the whole of the learned behavior of the group of known individuals could be understood—in the context of climate, the state of technology, and the degree of participation in other cultures.

Sociologists collected sets of responses to questionnaires employing large samples, and the analyses of the responses were handled in demographic and statistical contexts. Social psychologists used attitude scales, or questionnaires, or contrived laboratory situations with which to study human behavior. Historians, of course, worked with documents they were specially trained to interpret. Economists consulted data extracted from the economic life of the nation.

Sometimes, social scientists who worked with modern cultures rebuked anthropologists for wasting their energies on savages. There were occasional flurries of interest in such matters as minority group problems, immigration, and race relations. But for the most part, the mid-1930's gave little indication that anthropologists would contribute to the studies of cultures on a national level. There were exceptions, of course. Anthropologists could help by providing critical comment when a social scientist's interpretations were culture-bound and ethnocentric. They could also provide models for looking more attentively at local communities—as the Lynds had done in Middletown,[3] or as Lloyd Warner had done in the study of Yankee City.[4] In the early 1930's a group of young social scientists from twelve different countries was assembled at Yale University by Lawrence K. Frank, in the hope that by working together they could develop some applications of the new field of culture and personality to modern cultures. This seminar was premature but prophetic, and Lawrence Frank was one of the small group of people who inaugurated this approach when World War II provided the opportunity.

And so, at the beginning of that war, in asking ourselves what we could do on a national scale, we realized that we had two areas of competency. We had gained experience in thinking about whole societies, albeit they were sometimes very small. And we had experience in studying living human beings—especially as they developed from childhood to adulthood within different cultures. Our knowledge of remote parts of the world and our experience in living under exacting and exotic field conditions were also brought into play. Such knowledge and experience were essential in organizing stores of background knowledge on the South Sea Islanders, in preparing kits for airmen who might have to drop by parachute into the jungles of New Guinea, and in setting up courses in which the languages and cultures of other peoples were, for the first time, taught by teams of specialists. But the particular application with which I am concerned here is the work anthropologists did in predicting and interpreting the behavior of members of other nations, when they were acting as members of nations vis-à-vis other national groups.

Taking our experience in eliciting information from informants, and our knowledge of the way in which all aspects of cultural behavior are interrelated (mediated, as it is, by the individuals who embody it), we set out to explore those aspects of national behavior that could be assumed to be relevant because they were related to national institutions. This is the field of research that later came to be called the study of *national character*[5] and to the extent that research had to be done without access to the country being scrutinized, the study of *culture at a distance*.[6]

Our research involved interviews with members of the culture in which we were interested, interviews with members of other cultures who had spent years in the country under study, and intensive examination of cultural materials—particularly films,[7] novels, autobiographies, and diaries, which we could substitute for the kind of observation of life to which we were accustomed. We had to use our training in field work to help us identify behaviors that were characteristic of an entire nation (when acting in national and international contexts) and to judge to what extent a given piece of behavior, or any given cultural artifact, was idiosyncratic rather than representative. In so doing, we acted very much as practiced diagnosticians, depending upon experience that could neither be codified nor taught.

(This may help explain why the kind of work we did has not

been continued. For reasons I will discuss later, there has also been less demand for the contributions of anthropology at the policy-making level. But beyond this, the application of field work experience to the complexities of national and international relations demanded a considerable degree of maturity, of a kind that cannot be fabricated, and a skill, born of years of practice and not easily taught. Here anthropology shares with psychiatry a limitation on the contribution that can be made by the very recently trained young student. In both sciences, not only is experience a substitute for rigor, but a kind of clinical skill is equally involved.)

With Lawrence Frank acting as a kind of intellectual goad and entrepreneur, Ruth Benedict, Gregory Bateson, Geoffrey Gorer, Eliot Chapple, D. W. Lockard, and I, and later many other anthropologists, including Clyde Kluckhohn and Rhoda Metraux, took as our starting point the fact that wartime operations were being conducted primarily on or between national populations. People were involved—as members of armies, diplomats, as the audiences to wartime decrees, or the recipients of propaganda—as members of nation-states. Within these states, they differed enormously among themselves, by class, religion, region, and tribal affiliation. It was our task to find regularities in their behavior that could be attributed to national institutions—service in armies recruited nationally, response to national rationing or air raid regulations, and appeals to national images of bravery and sacrifice. Directives on such subjects came from national capitals and from propaganda beamed at other nations—friends or foes.

This need to concentrate on national behavior presented many problems, especially when we were dealing with European nations seen in all their complex historical diversity both by their own citizens and by many Americans. We presented what seemed like enormously oversimplified outlines of the way a people, as a people,[8] would respond to success or failure, would be stimulated by weakness or strength on the other side, would see themselves as hemmed in and surrounded, or would see themselves as eternally victorious even in defeat—forms of national behavior that were and are relevant to international relations. Students of history, and educated patriots, complain that we left out the great writers and poets and philosophers—that our framework was too narrow to include Goethe or Shakespeare. It was, indeed, too narrow, and it was meant to be. While the work of Goethe or Shakespeare is richer than the cultures on which they drew, in ways that made their works significant for later generations in countries other than their own, our outline of national character was less rich than the experience of any individual Englishman or German. Moreover, it did not allow for the complex historical differences between the different cultural versions of Normandy and Provence, between that of Bavaria and the Rhineland, between that of southern and northern England, or between New England and the southeastern United States. It was our task to exclude these richnesses and diversities in order to answer questions about the expected cruising range of Japanese war planes, or the responses of the English to the V-bombs, or how the Burmese would behave in a city set afire, or the Thais respond to pressure.[9]

This very necessary skeletonizing was a new scientific method, but unfortunately, it sometimes resembled very closely the folk-national stereotypes which the people of different nations have developed about each other, and about themselves. The education of the 1920's and 1930's had been aimed at discouraging stereotypic thinking, regardless of whether the stereotypes were or were not accurately drawn. Furthermore, the anthropological conception of regularities in behavior was, and still is, often mistaken for an insistence on nonexistent uniformities of behavior. (When we speak of regularities, we include clusters of positive and negative attitudes, and the absence of particular types of behavior as well as their presence in ways that are significantly interrelated. To give a very simple example, the necktie is an item of American male attire. An American male without a necktie is definitely underdressed in a way that a naked New Guinea mountaineer is not. Children who call their parents by their first names in a culture where kinship terms are the rule are doing something that is regularly related to those kinship terms. They are not—as they might be in another culture—simply using first names.)

The questions that we asked ourselves about each nation that we studied were not only limited to matters of war and peace, but were also primarily useful when the largest possible proportion of the population was involved. Thus, analyses of culturally relevant behavior applied more to those who were led than to the leader, to large armies more than to small forces, to the behavior of representative bodies like parliaments more than to randomly assembled groups. We were interested in whether a given people fought better when they were winning or when they were losing, or how people viewed compromise, and how great or how little capacity a people had to put themselves in other peoples' places. We were interested in the length of popular memory—in how long a response to a particular event could be elicited. (For example, Europeans continually overestimate the length of popular memory in the United States, and consequently act too soon, either as opponents or as allies, and are taken aback when the election results fail to reflect events six months old.)

Our studies were directed to the understanding of whole peoples, of the domestic appeals that would move them, and their responses as enemies or as allies. We used the same conceptual scheme to analyze ourselves and others, and because we were anthropologists and not psychiatrists, we dealt with the whole character of a people, their strengths as well as their weaknesses. This meant that we could in good conscience direct our sight toward those who were friends as well as toward those who were enemies, studying the responses of our own people as well as of others. The kind of knowledge that was needed is needed just as much for peacetime cooperation now as for wartime opposition then. What we learned from studies of the captured diaries of Japanese soldiers, or from Russian emigrés, is equally useful when the United States and Japan, or the United States and the Soviet Union, are pursuing some common goal.

I have been asked to present some examples of successes and failures in taking national culture and character into account in the conduct of international affairs. As these are nearly all selected from World War II, they have been documented elsewhere, and I shall not discuss them at length. The attitude of the Japanese toward displayed weakness had been diagnosed before Manila was declared an open city, and had this cultural diagnosis been used, we would not have attempted to save Manila by declaring it an open city. In so doing, we were relying on a European-like pride in shared treasures from a shared civilization, and upon the appeal of weakness to chivalry. We failed when we attempted to invoke such attitudes in the Japanese.

Furthermore, American planes were caught on the ground by the Japanese attack at the beginning of the war because Americans had made a faulty estimate of what the Japanese considered a feasible bombing distance. In the American view, this was seen as the distance a plane could fly to a target and return home again. To the Japanese, however, bombing distance did not necessarily involve the return trip. It was only later, but before the now famous *kamikaze* raids were known, that we were able to diagnose the very different Japanese attitudes toward war and the chances of return. Where Americans regarded death in war as bad luck, the Japanese treated a soldier leaving for war as already dead; his return was a piece of tremendous and unexpected good luck. This difference in attitude accounted for many miscalculations on the part of the Americans, until a better understanding of the Japanese could be built into our expectations.

In the area of Anglo-American relations, we were able to describe the contrast in the way in which the two English-speaking groups dealt with such problems as partnership.[10] The British treat a partnership much as if it were a tennis partnership for the duration of the game; the partners are assumed to be the same sort of people, and they boast and grieve for each other. But Americans think of a partnership as a sort of business partnership in which one partner has the brains and the other the money. Far from boasting about the other partner, each partner confides loudly that he has contributed the essential part to the success of the common venture. An understanding of these differences made it possible to smooth over many hurt feelings. The British experienced pained surprise in the way Americans responded when in a voice husky with emotion they whispered, "Hard luck about the Americans in Italy." They were no less surprised when, after they had given the Americans credit for anti-aircraft inventions which helped stop the buzz bombs, the Americans did not respond in kind as the British would have done. They did not compliment the British on the landing platforms which helped establish the Normandy beachhead, but instead boasted loudly in the national press, "American invention saves Britain." It was thus easy to understand why there had been so much negative response to Churchill's "Give us the tools and we'll finish the job" by Americans, who defined partnership as a situation in which one man has the money and the other has the skill and brains. We can understand, too, why Americans became so irate at the report that when an American confessed to an Englishman that "our statesmanship always comes out second best," the Englishman replied, "Of course we put it over on you— but not as often as we could."

During the war, it was useful to understand the difference between the British and American ideas of compromise. The British, acting from strength, would call a 95 per cent victory a pretty good compromise. But Americans, having won 95 per cent, would still complain that the other side had "pulled the wool over our eyes again." Later, when the Soviet Union was involved, it was necessary to include their attitude toward compromise as merely a strategic retreat whenever total victory was impossible.

Thus far, I have been discussing the kinds of explication of national character which, once elucidated, could inform national planning and facilitate international communications. A more specific type of anthropological contribution came from the proposal —made early in 1942—that we refrain from attacking the Japanese Emperor, as he would be needed at the end of the war to insure the complete surrender of a still militant Japan. This proposal, reiterated and strengthened by a large number of research workers, was in the end accepted because it could be made to the small command group. If, however, it had had to be debated in Congress, it would almost certainly have lost. Americans are too deeply convinced that monarchs of any sort are bad to have agreed to keep an emperor in power.

The success of this particular suggestion can be contrasted with the failure of suggestions made about the conduct of our relations with Germany after the surrender. We could, and did, prescribe that the Germans be left to deal with their own war criminals. We could, and did, prescribe that what was needed in Germany was a seasoned, mature army of occupation that could provide strong, fatherly, generous models of democratic leadership. None of these suggestions, culturally sound as they were, could be carried out. It did not accord with Anglo-American ethics, nor with our position vis-à-vis the Russians, to leave the Germans, who were ringed around by conquering armies, to settle their own scores. Instead of a seasoned army of men who had fought the Germans and who would not be overly impressed by the devastation wrought by Allied bombings, we sent in young, inexperienced, undisciplined new troops, who were as far as possible from the kind of occupation army that was indicated.

In all international affairs, one must take into account the national cultures of both sides. And often measures which may be best for one side, and ultimately for the world, may be quite unfeasible because of deeply ingrained attitudes of other nations or men involved. The advice about the Japanese Emperor would have failed if it had not been possible for a small group of men to rise above their national prejudices and take expert advice. We have as yet no way in which a whole people can be persuaded to take expert advice, least of all on their own cultural blind spots. I believe our experience during World War II, and immediately afterward, showed that cultural anthropological insights are most useful in wartime, when nations are deeply involved, if they can be presented to a small group with power to act. In peacetime, such studies contribute primarily to the formation of public opinion, to which government officials may, in turn, be responsive. But whereas in wartime government agencies may commission such studies, and are compelled to pay some attention to results, there is no single locus for such research in peacetime. Applied studies (and all of these studies are applied, for the conditions are too complex to provide ideal laboratories for research), always imply clients—someone on whose behalf research is undertaken. Research efforts like those commissioned in the 1940's and early 1950's leave a residue of organized knowledge and trained people who may be used as consultants and experts, but such a group's materials become progressively out of date. Although there may be an urgent need for contemporary insights similar to those found useful in wartime, there is no apparatus to achieve them.

I would now like to present two other areas where anthropological insights might have been used, but were not. One such failure occurred when the United States failed to realize the importance to emerging Indonesian identity of West New Guinea, now West Irian. Faced with different ways of thinking about the Indonesian demand for the inclusion of West Irian in the new nation, we let ourselves be pressured into thinking of the Indonesians as "brown imperialists." We could then disapprove of them thoroughly, instead of recognizing that the unity of the newly formed nation of Indonesia—like that of the original thirteen American colonies—depended upon *all* of the previous colonial holdings being kept together. In 1957 my Balinese informants asked, "If Irian does not belong to Indonesia, why do we?" By not recognizing the cultural legitimacy of Indonesia's claim to Irian, the United States lost an opportunity to oppose Indonesian expansion into territories not previously Dutch. This, of course, left us ethically powerless to oppose both the Indonesian military seizure of Irian, and the subsequent Indonesian expansionist measures.

There are many new complications in the use of cultural anthropology in policy making since we inaugurated the practice in 1941. The world is far more complicated; many of the nations whose behavior puzzles or bedevils the world today are so new that they cannot yet be said to have either a national culture or a national character. Instead of diagnosing an already deeply ingrained national character, as in the case of old nations like England,[11] Japan,[12] or France,[13] or even the United States and the U.S.S.R.,[14] we have to deal with attempts to build a national culture in nations like Indonesia and Nigeria. The methods we used on the older nations—methods which led to results that are still useful and valid in predicting the behavior, say, of the Soviet Union or of Great Britain—are not yet applicable to the new nations.

In many instances the older concerns of anthropologists with tribal or ethnic groups may again be relevant, especially in cases of rapid cultural change.[15] This was the case in the late 1940's, when a giant effort known as the Ground Nut program was launched in Africa. Natives of many different tribes were to be moved into new communities, and enough ground nuts planted to supply large parts of the world. The scheme hinged upon a proper organization of the migrants into an effective work force. Anthropological recommendations were that the various tribes from which the new work force was to be drawn be carefully studied, and that the tribe which already had a culture most nearly congruent with the demands of the scheme be selected, moved in first, and given time to establish a working style that members of later work forces could imitate. Instead, workers from many groups were rushed to the scene, and the whole plan was a fiasco.

In today's world, instead of working at home with a small selected group of highly representative informants and a variety of cultural products, it will be necessary to work in rapidly changing situations, such as now prevail in Papua-New Guinea, where over 500 languages are spoken.[16] The tides of world politics are sweeping these people into nationhood. There is urgent need to explore the potential strengths of a people who superficially present only a picture of political weakness. It is possible that peoples whose loyalty has extended only to its 500 or so members, and who regarded only another 500 or so as enemies, may have unplumbed possibilities for nationhood. But in today's climate of opinion, with the shades of project Camelot[17] still hanging over us, such research may become politically unfeasible. The sensitivities of just-emerging nations, on behalf of their own and similarly placed nations, may provide a greater barrier to the use of anthropological insight than did the offended pride of Europeans and Europeanphiles and their sentimental objections to all stereotyping in the 1940's.

Yet there remains one field in which there are inevitably a large number of clients, and to which anthropology can be applied—and that is to our own problems. To the extent that our own foreign affairs specialists really know something about American culture, they can do a better job—in diplomacy,[18] in foreign aid, in representing us to others, and in representing others to us. Comparative anthropological studies, in which insight is gained by the comparison of several cultures, remain our most reliable method of obtaining such insights into ourselves.[19] It should form a part of the curriculum of every school of international affairs.

Moreover, there is a parallel need for a new kind of anthropological training which will equip anthropologists to provide the kinds of materials that specialists in national and international affairs need. The traditional anthropological training has produced specialization by what are known as culture areas—geographical areas characterized by the primitive and exotic peoples who live within them, but excluding the modern inhabitants and modern governmental apparatuses of which they are a part. When a typical anthropologist goes into the field, he bypasses as much of the national and local government as possible, in order to get at his real material—groups of pygmies in the Ituri forests, or Eskimos in the far north, for example. These he studies intensively, but usually without working out the nexus between their contemporary state and the modern nations under whose sovereignty they live. Furthermore, the extensive preparation in the analysis of social structures that an anthropologist receives is designed to help him analyze kinship systems rather than modern bureaucracies; he is better equipped to deal with head-hunting feuds than with political parties. If he is to use his skill in analyzing culture in a way that is useful in the fields of government and international relations, he needs a different kind of training to replace our present dependence upon the acquisition of political sophistication simply by living a long time, thoughtfully.

I would suggest for the graduate work of the future that students who wish to contribute on a national or international scale specialize in manageable national units like Iran, the Republic of the Philippines, or Denmark. Within such nations there can be found primitive peoples, peasant peoples, and modern segments of society. Graduate students would thus find it of considerable value if the interrelationships of the subcultures and different regional and class versions of the national culture, and the relationship of the national culture to the rest of the world, came to be contained within their area of competence. Senior anthropologists of the old school often acquired such knowledge in the course of experience and were able to participate in national affairs and act as experts in fields of national planning. But if anthropologists are to make the large-scale contributions of which they are capable, there must be a form of training that is specifically relevant to such problems.

It will also be necessary—and this applies to the other social sciences too—to professionalize the field and distinguish between the training, the goals, the styles, and the rewards of the strictly academic vocations and the applied vocations. Just as physicians differ in their commitments from the academic scientists on whose researches they draw, so anthropologists who work on practical matters of contemporary political significance must be prepared to take a special stance. This will include such matters as forgoing publication in the interest of various sorts of political sensitivity, and a willingness to live at the same scale and in the same ways as those government officials who seek and take their advice. Some of the same commitment that is required of a physician or an educator who forgoes the acclaim of his fellows, and the rewards that come to one who devotes his life to research and publication, will be needed if we are to have career-applied political anthropologists who are capable of putting their disciplined knowledge, or ability to get such knowledge, quickly at the service of national and international political units.

The task is much more complicated today, but we also have much faster communication, better facilities for research, better conceptual schemes and computers. There are too many countries that must be considered at once for anyone to handle in his head, but it is possible to program a large number of special variables, including expected reaction time to foreign news; standard responses to certain other nations as rivals or former colonial governors; peculiarities of current leaders; and strength of the party in power, as well as the more stable cultural variables, such as response to defeat or victory. Combining the new instruments with a new sort of education, both for those who are preparing for international relations and for those who are preparing to be a new kind of cultural anthropologist, should give us a useful and sensitive instrument for analyzing world situations,[20] implementing national policy and promoting world order. We could begin by learning something relevant about Vietnam.

7

THE ROLE OF GROUPS:
CONTRIBUTIONS OF SOCIOLOGY

Lewis Coser
Brandeis University

M uch social theorizing, until fairly recently, seems to have been dominated by what the great German sociologist, Georg Simmel, once called the "fallacy of separateness." It was assumed that the social world consists of separate individuals striving to maximize their self-interests or, insofar as politics is concerned, to choose rationally, as self-conscious citizens, among the various alternatives available in a particular area of policy.

This Robinson Crusoe interpretation of political action increasingly has come to be rejected in the study of man and his society. It has been accepted, by and large, that any explanation of human behavior must start with the recognition that man is a social and political animal, powerfully affected by his interaction with others. John Dewey said it better than I can:

> The human being whom we fasten upon as individual *par excellence* is moved and regulated by his association with others; what he does and what the consequences of his behavior are, what his experience consists of, cannot even be described, much less accounted for, in isolation.[1]

This view implies a very decisive shift in the perspective that is brought to bear on the analysis of political behavior in general and of international relations in particular. It is no longer possible, for example, to adhere to the image of the ideal-typical citizen which is implied in classical democratic theory. According to this view, to quote Lord Bryce,

> ... every citizen has, or ought to have, thought out for himself certain opinions, i.e., ought to have a definite view, defensible by argument, of what the country needs, of what principle ought to be applied in governing it, of the men to whose hands the government ought to be entrusted.[2]

Yet even a superficial view of how the business of politics is actually conducted, of how opinions are formed, communicated, and crystallized into political decisions will readily show that this is an assumption which is nowhere even approximately fulfilled. Men's views are products of the associations they form with others. The family, school, neighborhood, and peer group form and mold the personality of the child. He learns in these face-to-face groups to define himself in relation to the world that surrounds him, and his attitudes and values, including his political views, are powerfully shaped in these early encounters with others who are of significance to him. Political socialization begins, so to speak, in the nursery school. Certain styles of behavior—predispositions, say, to authoritarian or permissive styles in interpersonal relations—may already be firmly grounded in very early childhood encounters with significant others. These styles will help govern later political attitudes.

Yet, lest we succumb to the untenable assumption that all of man's destiny is already firmly decided in the nursery school, we must hasten to add that even though certain interpersonal attitudes may be partly formed in the early stage of life, they come to be further molded, and remolded, in later years. Though the term socialization—the process by which a person learns to become a member of his society—is often used to refer only to the early stages of a man's life, a better usage of the concept refers to changes in the individual throughout his life cycle. The variety of groups with which a man affiliates in his mature life—his occupational group, his political associations, his religious or class belongingness —all determine in some measure the kind of man he is. His attitudes and behavior, the ways he perceives the world around him, are shaped and filtered through the group contexts in which he moves. "A man's social life," wrote William James, "is the recognition he gets from his mates." The human self is now commonly seen to mature in and through commerce with others. It is in the context of social acts that the self arises. Group experiences "give the individual, either directly, or by sanctioning or censoring attitudes and behaviors stemming from isolated individual experiences, a general outlook, or frame of reference, in terms of which he perceives and evaluates events."[3]

What has been said so far by way of introduction constitutes the bare bones of what may be termed a sociological perspective. While this perspective is widely shared in regard to political behavior generally, much thinking about international relations still seems to be dominated by two different points of view which, though seemingly opposed, seem to me to share in common a reliance on the assumption of human separateness. I refer to what, for want of a better term, I shall call the "theory of an undifferentiated public," and to "elite theory."

In the first theory no effort is made to distinguish various groups and subgroups or divisions within the polity; it is assumed that raw public opinion data on how Frenchmen or Americans feel about certain issues provide the best indicators for intelligent foreign policy. In this view it is often assumed, for example, that "war begins in the minds of men," so that, if we contribute to better understanding between people and help reduce the stereotypical notions which becloud the minds of ordinary citizens, we can reduce the sources of clash and conflict on the international scene. Such a view fails to acknowledge, it may be noted in passing, that if we really understood the springs of action of an antagonist we might dislike him more rather than less—some nations, like some people, might not improve upon acquaintance. Even more importantly, it assumes that public opinion is essentially the product of a simple process of addition of private opinions formed by an essentially undifferentiated public. This, however, is not the case. Opinions must be sociologically placed if we are to reason intelligently about political behavior.[4]

Opinions and attitudes must be located in the social and political structure. For example, in analyzing United States-Canadian relations, it will not do to rest the case on a finding that, say, a given percentage of Canadians favor closer relations with the United States. Raw figures begin to make sense only when we discover that attitudes toward the United States, like any other attitudes, will differ considerably once we consider such factors as class belongingness, regional differentiation, or ethnic identity. For example, fairly high proportions of Canadian workers and lower class persons indicated in public opinion polls that they would have no objection to Canada becoming a part of the United States.

But such sentiments tended to decline as one moved from the lower to the higher rungs of the social ladder. Here it is important to realize that even a relatively small absolute number of upper class persons can express and maintain the dominant conservative point of view, even though it may not be shared by a great number in the underlying population.

This structural factor has also to be considered in conjunction with ethnic differences. High proportions of the upper and professional classes of French Canada favor a greater degree of autonomy and even eventual independence of Quebec from the rest of Canada while the working class of French Canada seems much less inclined in this direction. In this case the traditionalist lower class would have to be won over by a more dynamic and innovating upper class if its political perspective were to get the upper hand. The constellation of forces in Canada becomes even more complex once we realize that western Canada as a whole has a much more favorable and positive image of the United States than is the case in the east.

Thus it is not so much numbers of private individuals who decide the political direction of a society as the interplay between persons holding different positions in the class, ethnic, and regional structures of the country. Hence, in this case, as in many others, information relevant to the making of policy must include knowledge of the social and political structure and processes. We must be aware of the ways in which men's affiliations with various groups—class, occupation, ethnic collectivities, or regions—affect their outlook and orientations, and how these orientations balance or tilt the power constellations.

Let me turn now to the second view, which takes an opposite stance from the first one. While the first view is most often taken by men of humanitarian and liberal predispositions in the international as well as the national arena, the second is usually associated with a "hard" view of international and national "reality." The "hard line" asserts that there is no need to be particularly concerned with the opinions of the bulk of a nation's population, that this "democratic myth" must be discarded and that the opinions of only a relatively small elite have any policy implications. In this view societal power is always held by a relatively small minority since the very structure of any complex society and organization prevents the mass from exercising power. Hence only those who occupy positions at the summit in the economy, in government, in political, religious, and military organizations as well as in education and the professions need to be taken into consideration in the conduct of international affairs. The rest form but an ineffective chorus while the actions of the high and the mighty make policy and shape the future. This position usually prides itself on its superior realism and treats condescendingly what it considers the "soft" humanitarian idealism of the first.

This view rests on the fallacy of separateness twice compounded. It is not so much that it also deals with individual persons—this time members of the elite—making individual decisions; but these men are held to be separate from the rest of their society, as if they were not subject to support or opposition, as the case may be, from different groups in that society. Groupings with separate economic, political, social, and moral interests and with differential power exist within any society. To be sure, in periods of political and social stability the power elite may well be the sole determinant group of men. But stability may not always or even usually prevail. The elite theory is indeed wedded to the ideal of social stability. Elite theorists tend to reason that those who are momentarily in positions of dominance will necessarily continue to be in such positions. They extrapolate, in other words, from a balance of power and influence at the present moment in time to its continuation in the future. And that leads to their analytical weakness.

Elite theorists fail to take into account that the politics of the twentieth century are politics of instability. The elitist view might have made considerable sense in an age when traditionalist ideology still maintained the societal hierarchy, and when only a small elite had effective decision-making power. It becomes inapplicable in our times, when masses of men hitherto mute have entered the political arena, when elites are met by counterelites and traditional cultures by countercultures. In our times, men located in a variety of positions in the social structure may suddenly attain a power voice in the polity. Under modern circumstances, political and social change, as well as stability, may derive not so much from the policies of elites as from many crisscrossing alliances between economic interest groups; not so much from decisions taken by a few powerful men as from compromises arrived at by the most disparate groups holding the most disparate values and attitudes.

But what is perhaps even more important is that groups of men hitherto unheard of may consolidate their forces and form a new source of power. Embarrassment might have been spared American policy-makers, and especially the dominant political and social strata in the South, had it been foreseen that the Negro population would soon become a major political force. Exclusive concern with tradition-oriented political behavior, and insufficient attention to political processes among groups excluded at the moment from the exercise of power but able tomorrow to realize claims to leadership, may lead to blindness in political perception, to miscalculation in international decision-making, and to political impotence.

Nor does it suffice to say that these newly emerging groups are themselves but appendices of an existing elite. As a case in point, take the situation of a number of so-called "new nations" which only recently achieved independence. The men who now exercise power in these nations do not originate, in most cases, from the traditional elite strata. The leaders of most African nations are not descendants of tribal chiefs or royal lines. They emerged, by and large, from a very small layer of Westernized or semi-Westernized men, professionals or semiprofessionals. They are intellectuals or semi-intellectuals. They were but recently starving students at the London School of Economics or at the Sorbonne, or obscure union organizers in some provincial backwater. And they made the move from obscurity to elite visibility within but a few years. One is reminded in this respect of the possibly apocryphal story of some Viennese political analysts, around 1916, discussing, around a cafe table, the likelihood of a revolution in Russia. Said the skeptical colleague to his more sanguine partner, "And who do you suppose would lead the revolution? Perhaps that Mr. Bronstein-Trotzki who used to play chess at the next table. . . ."

There are, of course, certain indices which may be consulted, particularly in the new nations, for help in identifying future leaders. If I had been asked, ten years ago, in Zanzibar, or Tanganyika, or some such place, whence the future leadership might come, I certainly would have asked in turn, "Which people in the past ten years have had exposure to the London School of Economics? What types of people have been out of the country? What types of people have been able to compare local situations with situations in a wider context?" I would have raised the question of what we often call "relative deprivation," meaning that it is not those who are absolutely deprived or frustrated who are likely to play a major role in a political movement, but rather those who have had a chance to compare their lot with that of comparable but better-off people in some other society. Then I would have launched a study in greater depth of the groups thus identified. Clearly, you couldn't have said, "This man and that man will be leading the government

ten years hence"; but I think you could have said that the leadership
will come from such and such strata or occupational groupings,
rather than from others.

It is argued, furthermore, that no matter what their origins, the
present decision-makers represent the effective elite toward whom
the foreign policy-makers ought to be oriented now. One may
immediately counter that they may be displaced tomorrow by yet
a different group of men emerging, say, through the military establishment. The obscure sergeants of today may well be the generals
and national leaders of tomorrow.

Not only do new, hitherto unnoticed groups suddenly emerge
on the political scene, not only do their leaders frequently come
from other strata than from yesterday's elite, it is also insufficient
to argue, as I did earlier, that the elite depends for its own survival
on support from and compromises with nonelite strata. It ought
to be added that as the masses have increasingly invaded the political arena, the societal potential for revolution has increased. If
this be so, it follows that major analytical attention needs to be
focused on, among others, actual or potential revolutionary actors,
their objectives, and the responses they achieve.[5]

Far from relying on a somewhat domesticated and tame vision
of social and political structure according to which relevant political acts are expected, by and large, to come from the elite
holders of legitimate power, we must accustom ourselves to a view
of political process which is ever alert to the inherent possibility,
often perhaps amounting to a probability, that power will be accumulated and mobilized in other than elite strata and that revolutionary actors may take over a scene hitherto dominated by an
old and now somewhat superannuated cast.

From this it would seem to follow that we need to be concerned
not only with the recruitment and socialization of present elites
but also with sources for the recruitment of counterelites, not only

with the smooth flow of power in an institutionalized political structure but also with the disruption of this flow through the sudden emergence of new power centers or the penetration of hitherto inarticulate strata into the structure of politics. We cannot limit ourselves to a consideration of how political decisions are presently arrived at but must construct imaginative models on how the decision-making process might be upset or modified if new political actors appeared on the scene. Let me give just two examples:

1. Few American decision-makers about international affairs seem to have been prepared for the significant shifts in French foreign policy that followed the accession of General de Gaulle to the presidency. They assumed that, by and large, though the personal style of de Gaulle would make some difference, French policy would in the main follow the traditional path of the Third and Fourth Republics. They failed to see, however, that the Gaullist takeover of power brought in its wake a new, more technocratically oriented and more nationalistic group of policy-makers and high-level bureaucrats. Had attention been paid to the orientation, the training, and the recruitment of this new alternative elite, their responses, once they had come into positions of power, would have been somewhat more predictable.

2. Similarly, exclusive concentration on the ruling elites made it almost impossible for those in charge of American foreign relations to get an understanding of the process through which masses and competing elites alike undermined the legitimate structure of many Latin American countries. One ventures to think that the disaster of American policy in relation to Cuba might have been avoided had some serious insight been gained about the process through which large strata of middle class professionals were alienated from Batista's regime, about how alternative leadership was gradually being generated in the universities, and about

how an initially small group of professional revolutionaries managed, within a few years, to undermine and overthrow the previous
Cuban polity.

The view I am trying to advance here sees political actions in
both domestic and external affairs to be the resultant of a process
in which a variety of groups, both elite and nonelite, play a major
part. Many of these groups are organized and represent specific
economic and value orientations and interests. Others may only
be potential groups not presently organized but susceptible of becoming organized under propitious conditions.

De Tocqueville shrewdly observed in *Democracy in America*,
that,

> In democratic countries . . . it frequently happens that a great num-
> ber of men who wish or who want to combine cannot accomplish it
> because as they are very insignificant and lost amid the crowd, they
> cannot see and do not know where to find one another. . . .[6]

Such pluralistic ignorance, de Tocqueville observed, might be
overcome with the help of newspapers. With his customary
shrewdness he put his finger on a major political factor which has
assumed even more importance in our day than it possessed in his.
The effective activation of unorganized interests into self-conscious
and politically effective groups depends upon the accessibility of
means of communication. These means of communication, therefore, have a central place in the sociological analysis of social and
political structures. More particularly, as long as all channels of
communication are effectively controlled by the governing elite
groups, these can to a large extent prevent the formation of counterelites or organized groups voicing the demands of hitherto unrecognized interests. But when alternate channels of communication become publicly available to alienated individuals, they may
help to mobilize hitherto unrecognized and unorganized interests.

In democratic nations the channels of communication, while not completely open, are yet typically open enough to allow and facilitate the expression of the rival claims of even those groups which may be excluded from direct access to the sources of power. In such nations freedom of speech and of the press as well as freedom of assembly provide available mechanisms for the activation of unorganized interests.[7] And although in countries which do not enjoy a democratic polity—and let us not forget that this includes today most of the new nations—such channels of free expression are not provided for those who may wish to dissent from official policy or who want to press for the recognition of hitherto ignored interests, a variety of informal or even illegal means of communication may be used in order to activate hitherto unorganized or even suppressed interests.

Hence, in such countries it would be a major mistake to assess the situation by paying exclusive attention to the officially controlled channels of communication. The study of these needs to be complemented by attention to what is said in coffee houses and in the bazaars and what may be written in clandestine sheets. If this is not attended to, the danger is great that a heavily distorted picture of the real situation is relayed to the policy-makers. Had there been more information, for example, about what people actually said to each other in Saigon cafes and peasant village assemblies, Washington policy-makers might have received a less distorted view of the Diem regime in South Vietnam. Had there been better information on what people thought and said about Castro's regime before the disaster of the Bay of Pigs, Washington policy-makers might not have fallen into the disastrous error of believing that the people of Cuba were ready to rise against Castro once the news of the landing reached them. Had more attention been paid in many new nations to the language of the market place, of the student assemblies, and of the village square, it might have been possible to detect incipient signs of disaffection, alienation, and withdrawal from official politics which eventually led to the revolutionary emergence of new political groups and new political leadership.

Hans Morgenthau once remarked in his characteristically blunt manner that:

> When it comes to evaluating the actual or potential power of a nation, the diplomatic mission takes on the aspects of a high-class and *sub rosa* spy organization. . . . In this function of gathering information upon which the foreign policy of one's own country could be founded, lies the root of modern diplomacy.[8]

The information relayed by Foreign Service officers and their ancillary personnel to the centers of foreign policy-making provides the raw materials for decisions. The output of such decisions, it stands to reason, is dependent on the input in information. If diplomacy is unable to assess correctly the objectives of other nations and the effective power at their disposal, the resultant policy decisions are likely to be faulty. I do not wish to assert that adequate information guarantees good policy—we have come a long way from the nineteenth-century utilitarian view that only ignorance and error prevent men from always coming to conclusions beneficial to the commonweal. But adequate information is clearly a necessary, if not sufficient, condition for intelligent policy choice.

In earlier periods of history such gathering of information was a relatively uncomplicated affair. When, in the sixteenth century, permanent diplomatic missions began to replace the system of special envoys to foreign countries, it was assumed, and correctly so, that all the relevant information could be gathered in the capital city and in the courts. Since, in the age of absolutism, power was highly concentrated and since only a very small stratum of men constituted the effective decision-making body, diplomatic information could restrict itself to what was happening in these limited circles. Matters changed, of course, when, after the democratic revolutions, other strata in the population became relevant to political decision-making. Hence the nineteenth-century diplomat had to concern himself with several strategic elites and publics, and with more complex issues. Decisions taken, say, at a meeting of merchants in Manchester or of trade union officials on the Clydeside could have deep-going implications for British foreign policy. Shifts in public opinion vis-à-vis Ireland could be of decisive importance for the alignment of forces in Westminster and for the policies of Whitehall. Fleet Street and Transport House might be more important for the gathering of policy-relevant information than Downing Street.

Yet even in the more pluralistic politics of the nineteenth century the tasks of the diplomat were still relatively uncomplicated. Power was now more dispersed, publics had become more differentiated and elites more varied; yet the alignments on the political arena were still relatively stable—at least when one compares them to the politics which have emerged in the twentieth century. This is why the nineteenth-century diplomat could still rely, by and large, on his own resources, in his attempts to assess the situation in a foreign country. And this is why he needed only a minimum of ancillary and specialized personnel in order to help him in his assessment.

In our age, just as intelligent planning and action on the domestic scene have become impossible without recourse to a great number of experts and specialists, so on the international scene the complexity of the task of information-gathering requires, I would contend, much greater reliance on specialized and expert help.

The information input required in our day to come to intelligent decisions cannot be provided by men relying on common sense alone—though it might be remarked in passing that, as one surveys a series of decisions in American foreign policy in recent years, one cannot escape the impression that a bit more common sense would often have come in handy.

For instance, anthropologists will be needed to assess the influence of tribal organizations or family structure on political organization and recruitment of personnel in a new nation. That anthropologists may also be consulted to good effect by policy-makers concerned with developed nations of ancient culture was demonstrated during World War II. A group of brilliant cultural anthropologists working in Washington recommended the retention after the war of the Japanese Emperor as a symbolic, if not an actual, power figure. The advice was heeded; and it turned out later to have been very important advice indeed.

Social psychologists will be needed to assess trends in public opinion and shifts in attitudes and values. Economists will have to assess productivity and labor-market developments. Some of the best economists have been part-time sociologists. Joseph Schumpeter was the first to point to entrepreneurs as a key group in national development. He was concerned with entrepreneurs in the Western context. Now everyone recognizes they are also crucial to development in Latin America or India.

Demographers will be needed to assess population trends and their not only on national power but also on economic development. Political scientists will help assess the formal and informal shifts in the domestic balance of power, and military experts will have to gauge the state of military preparation. Sociologists, I would suggest in concluding, deserve a place in this team. They can bring to it their particular skills in the investigation of all those associational and group factors, from studies of elites to studies of the underlying population, from studies of the mass media and other channels of communication to studies in the system of stratification and the allocation of power, status, and resources. And in addition to their more specialized contributions, they will, let us hope, be able to contribute a more holistic view of total society, a picture of the way in which the various parts of the society and its various institutions fit together in some functional totality in which all parts affect one another and are in turn affected by the whole. Of particular importance to the holistic view of society and to national development in general may be the marginal groups in the population.

During a two-week trip to Mexico I was much impressed by the importance of the roles being played there by various minority groups; in Mexico City a tiny band of Spanish Republicans has a disproportionate place in the cultural and economic life of the capital, and a very small group of Jews is enormously important. In mapping the population of a new nation one should early seek out such marginal minorities, who, precisely because they lack security, may be impelled to innovate—culturally, economically, or even politically.

The social perceptions in regard to foreign affairs of those in power and authority can be influenced by social scientists calling attention to previously neglected problems and issues. Social scientists can also usefully point out to the policy-makers that all men generally have certain set ideas which come mainly out of their own experience and which influence their perception of any foreign policy situation. Mexican sociologists I met were unanimously convinced that United States policy in Vietnam was wrong, not because they had looked at the facts of the Vietnamese situation, but because "the North Americans impose their will on small countries." How to change the general Mexican optic is a difficult question, but it is a very important question.

Yet it would be an indulgence in unwarranted Comtean optimism to assume that enlightenment will at all times be sufficient to alert the powerful. They often lack sensitivity while the sensitive often lack power. Two areas where men of power might profitably become more sensitive are in transferring institutions and demanding greater public support of the powerful nations' policies and actions. Sociologists might help puncture the illusion that you simply can take a Western parliamentary system and impose it on Nigeria or Ghana and expect it to function.

Historically, the most successful transferral of institutions has resulted from selective borrowing. The example of Japan might well make a better model for developing countries today than the former colonial mother countries.

Those in authority should also recognize the necessity for leaders in the new nations to reconcile what they say to America with their statements to home audiences. These leaders may wish to institute a dialogue with America or the West; and simultaneously, they may have to defend traditional values at home. This ambivalence is characteristic even of developed, Western nations in their relations with us. European sociologists are wont to express distaste for "American methods"—quantitative analyses, IBM machines, and other tools of the modern sociologist. Then, after defending their national integrity, they may inquire as to the possibilities for obtaining a fellowship or visiting professorship in the United States. Pointing out their technological backwardness would exacerbate their defense reactions and end the dialogue. It is best to concede their general argument, then move on to consider the advantages of the use of computers in solving particular problems.

Although men of knowledge and men of power have seldom found it easy to communicate, communicate they must if we are not to enter an age where mindless power confronts powerless minds. May I close with a quote from a man whom I consider, alongside Machiavelli, the father of the modern realistic study of man and his society: Thomas Hobbes. "No man," he wrote in his *Behemoth*, "can have in his mind a conception of the future, for the future is not yet. But of our own conceptions of the past [and I would add, of the present—L.C.] we make a future."[9]

8

PSYCHOLOGY AND PSYCHOLOGICAL OPERATIONS

Daniel Lerner
Massachusetts Institute of Technology

Naturally, not all individuals play the same kind of role in international relations. For our purposes, we can separate the roles into four categories.

The most important group is composed of the elites—those who make the decisions and direct the operations which govern relations among nations. There is no question that these individuals—government officials and those who influence their decisions—are of the greatest significance.

In the second group is the participant public—those who have an operational interest in international relations and who occasionally have some influence on decisions. In this group are international businessmen; the international press corps, whose business it is to make international relations exciting to the public and to inform that public; officials of international labor union organizations; officials of international student organizations, who sometimes coordinate their activities for political effect; and additional subgroups who have a professional interest in international affairs and who sometimes exert pressure on the conduct of international relations.

I would call the third group the attentive public. These are people who read the newspapers, listen to the radio, and think that what's happening outside of their own community or own country is as important as what's happening inside. They have at least a casual interest in what's going on, but normally they have no influence on what happens. This is still a fairly small group within the population at large.

Finally, in the fourth category, there remains in most countries, including this one, the large public that is not related to international relations or international affairs or politics in any significant way. They have little or no interest or influence. I want to concentrate on this group that is not terribly interested and does not have any direct influence on what happens in the normal course of relations between nations.

I am afraid that some psychologists have seriously misled us into attributing too much importance to the role of this mass public in international relations. The error is rather basic and it is built into much of contemporary psychologizing. I don't know how we shall rid psychology of this error until psychologists take a fresh look at the "democratic assumption," with particular reference to international relations.

The democratic assumption of psychology, which is quite valid for scientific purposes in laboratories and classrooms, is that any individual is just as interesting and important to study as any other.

This assumption is quite tenable if you want to study perception, attention, cognition, or other particular ways of interacting with the environment. Because the assumption holds in these situations, some psychologists have tended to assume that all individuals may be treated as equals in whatever situations they study.

By a curious transmutation, the assumption has attached itself to a specific political model—a "democratic model" of international relations—where the operating rules are that every head has a vote and that any vote is as good as any other in the final tabulation. Now, for some purposes (although not, probably, for most) such a democratic model can be useful. Where it becomes terribly misleading, and indeed becomes the "democratic fallacy," is in the analysis of international relations.

In relations among nations, the great mass of the people in any country does not play a significant role, just as in international relations some nations are stronger than other nations. To a psychologist, all striated muscles may be equally worthy of study. Those who would understand international relations, however, must recognize at the start that weaker muscles do not have the same importance as stronger ones. Nor does the nonparticipant population of a country count as much as its decision-makers.

As an example, let me cite a study that took many thousands of dollars, several years, and the energies of some very good psychologists. I refer to the tensions project sponsored by UNESCO shortly after World War II. This project was based on one of the key sentences in the UNESCO Charter: "Wars begin in the minds of men." The project was supposed to grow out of this idea; and it was designed to study the tensions that cause wars. Those who performed the study did not stop long enough to ask: which wars? which men? which minds? If they had, they would have been led to conclude that very few wars have started in anybody's mind; the minds in which wars have started belonged to very few men.

Wars are not the result of popular tensions; and it would be very hard to find instances of wars which could be properly attributed to tensions among individuals.

Tensions, as an analytic category of social psychology, are twentieth-century phenomena—as, indeed, is analytic social psychology itself. Tensions in this sense tend to be either a result of negotiations between leaders of countries or induced consequences of hostile relationships. The tensions don't cause the wars; the tensions sometimes accompany wars. They are either produced by the media, or induced by the leadership, or both. But it is a gross error to assume that wars—one extreme class of international relations—are caused by tensions or by what goes on in the minds of most men.

Having been so blunt up to this stage, I must now introduce a caution. The democratic fallacy does not disqualify democratic theory from any role in the study of international relations. Nor is it my intention to introduce an antidemocratic fallacy, which would be just as serious an analytical error and possibly a more grievous ideological error.

To stress the errors of some psychologists is not to exclude, or even to constrain, psychology from playing any role in the study of international relations. But it is necessary to point out why the work of many professional psychologists in the international field has been unproductive. They have failed to take account of the fact that the elite of international relations—those who make decisions and conduct foreign policy and international negotiations—are very different from the participant and the attentive public, who enter into the process in one indirect way or another. The influence of both the participant and the attentive public, indeed, is usually no greater than their influence upon the decision-maker. Even this modicum is greater than the influence of the nonparticipant, and usually apathetic, mass of people.

Let us turn, by way of illustration, to some cases in which the mass does participate. They participate whenever international relations are in crisis. Mainly, the mass participates in time of war and of revolution.

The categorization of revolution presents a difficult problem. It tends, in historical writings, to be interpreted as a kind of war. Consider briefly the three major revolutions of modern Western history. The American Revolution, which was conducted against an external enemy that had been the colonizing power, has since been rebaptized the War of Independence. We don't teach our children any more to consider what happened in 1776 as a revolution. We teach them to think of it as a war of independence, rather akin to the wars of liberation we see all over the world today. The French Revolution, which was conducted against an internal enemy, has since been reinterpreted as a civil war—a war conducted entirely within the confines of a single nation against a segment of a national population. The most important example, and the hardest to classify, is the Bolshevik Revolution, which was conducted against an ideological enemy defined as both external and internal. That is perhaps the truest modern example we have of a revolutionary war, and we still don't know what to make of it in historical terms. It is clear, however, that the mass of people was involved in each case. The important thing about the mass being involved in the revolutions—the factor that may explain why revolutions are now reinterpreted as wars—is that the mass gets involved only in warlike situations where it is needed to fight.

Let us look next at the example of war. Since at least the time of Napoleon, in the French *levée en masse*, we have seen the development of mass armies. In World War I, a hundred years later, the Germans developed the theory of the nation in arms. Surrounding this theory, with all its conventionalized Germanic psychological and sociological overtones, was the notion that people have to be involved ideologically and morally in all sorts of intense relationships with foreign policy. Basic to this notion was the fact that modern war required mass armies. In World War II, the whole notion of the nation in arms took a somewhat different turn, a turn to the "left," when the United States developed the theory of the democratic crusade. General Eisenhower called it a Crusade in Europe. Out of this came two kinds of consequences which are very relevant to the role of the individual in international relations. For one thing, if you are leading a democratic crusade, you must somehow satisfy your followers that their interests are being served. During World War II historically unprecedented and massive efforts of propaganda took place, beginning with the armed forces. The men who were fighting had to remain convinced that this was their war.

This "new army" in the United States was a very important consequence of propaganda, just as propaganda itself grew out of American society. Let me focus on three developments within the American army during World War II as examples of the kinds of things which can happen when individuals participate in the conduct of international relations in the special case of war.

Continuous studies were being made during World War II of American soldiers, marines, and airmen. After the war these studies were brought together in the monumental volumes entitled *The American Soldier*. In this work you will find described in detail three transformations of major proportion in the United States armed forces.

In the mass, citizen army a revolutionary idea was introduced: not only did soldiers have a right to gripe, but they should be allowed to gripe in public; within military channels, they should be allowed to send their gripes over the heads of their commanding officers. The gripes were made public in the soldiers' newspaper, the *Stars and Stripes*. Through the institution of the unendorsed letter to the Inspector General, any soldier who had a complaint could direct it in writing to the highest level, without having his letter scrutinized by officers in his chain of command. These two innovations produced a communications revolution in the United States armed forces.

It was the communication wedge that led to a complete transformation of social relations in the army, navy, and air force. To Americans today it seems almost unbelievable that, before World War II, officers and enlisted men were not allowed to fraternize. They could not eat a meal together, they couldn't be seen in any kind of social relation with each other. All of this sounds like Britain in the eighteenth century, but it was true in this country in 1942. It was less true in 1943, and it was practically ended by 1945.

Finally, I would remind you that the first real progress in achieving equality in civil rights came as a result of wartime and postwar orders by President Roosevelt and President Truman to begin integration of Negro and white troops and open up promotions for Negroes in the armed forces.

I submit that all of these transformations illustrate what can be done in situations where the mass public and the individual nonelite citizens count for something in the conduct of international relations.

But important as these developments were, the point of mobilizing American forces in World War II was not to revolutionize the social structure in the United States but to beat the Germans, Italians, and Japanese. What did we learn in our World War II psychological operations against enemy soldiers about the role of the individual in international relations and our ability to influence enemy soldiers' individual decisions?

I was personally involved in psychological operations against Germany. I assume we did pretty well, because we won the war at low military cost to us and at a high psychological cost to the Germans. We also learned a good deal about the limitations of psychological warfare and about some of its unanticipated effects on the psychological warriors.

The operations of psychological warfare during World War II were designed to subvert the German army, the Wehrmacht. The idea was to accomplish this by undermining its morale, its cohesion, and its will to fight. Among the Germans, as among the Americans, this was an instance where the individual counted very heavily, because he had to do the fighting.

Among the things we learned from this experience was that ideological argumentation turned out to be practically worthless. You couldn't argue ideologically with the German soldier and accomplish anything operational. As a matter of fact, one of the rules of tactical psychological warfare came to be: don't argue with them! Never write anything into a leaflet or a radio script that is intended to convert them to your ideas.

I think that this is important. It illustrates why the individual has such a limited role in international relations. In our intelligence studies of Wehrmacht morale we developed an acid test for whether an individual was surrender-prone; this test was the index of loyalty to Hitler. We learned this by questioning prisoners. We questioned them so much that by the time we were through with them I imagine that many of them wished they were back in the combat zone. But it turned out that if a soldier had sworn an oath of loyalty to Hitler, there was little our propaganda could do that would seriously affect his ideological, moral, or political attitude-structure.

As a corollary to this we devised the idea of teaching German soldiers how to "help themselves"—i.e., how to surrender. We didn't try to persuade anybody to accept any idea, but merely how to save himself. The most important thing we did in tactical psychological warfare was "greasing skids." If a fellow was on the skids, we just put a little grease on them. We didn't try to convert him to anything, we didn't teach him anything except how to do more efficiently what he wanted to do anyway. We did such things as produce a Safe Conduct pass, in which the only text was instruction on how to say "I surrender" in phonetic English. Now when this is the most successful kind of propaganda—and it was—which you can use when individuals are most heavily engaged, most participant, I submit that we need to reconsider all of our ideas about the use of psychology on individuals in international relations, whether in peace or war, whether in revolution or nonviolent change. Otherwise, some of our simple notions based on a fallacious view of democracy are very misleading and can only do us harm.

I shall not attempt to forecast the long-term effects of this surrender propaganda in World War II. But I submit that the postwar Germans, especially the veterans of Allied psychological warfare, have been much more docile than the veterans after World War I. No one, to my knowledge, has studied systematically the postwar effects of our surrender propaganda on the Germans. But it is clear that no "stab-in-the-back" legend is abroad in Germany today. My guess is that too many corporals surrendered with their sections, too many sergeants with their platoons, to be able to give credibility, even to themselves, to any such claim. I would speculate that the lingering guilt among Germans is due to the effectiveness of Allied, and particularly American, surrender propaganda.

What about the consequences for those who waged this propaganda? When I was preparing a study of psychological warfare, I wrote a letter to many of the people who had been in this business with me and asked how they evaluated the effectiveness of various themes and techniques. They wrote back with many different interpretations and emphases. But one answer impressed me greatly. It was from a leaflet writer, a very thoughtful one, who wrote: "For me, it was a psychological Hiroshima." This has stayed in my mind, because it seems to me that in seeking to influence individuals, we go into the most risky, the most dangerous, the most unreliable, and the most unstudied phase of international relations. Everybody who is conservative, and in this sense I am, prefers that international relations be conducted by governments. All radical movements seek to bypass governments by operating directly on individuals. My word of warning, as a psychological conservative, is that when one tries to bypass government and diplomacy, with its fairly standardized techniques of international communication, one lets loose mechanisms and activates processes which we don't understand very well.

I think, perhaps, that instead of taking as my last illustration a dramatic one, like what's being done in Vietnam, I might take a more peaceful situation. It is particularly important for Americans to start worrying about this situation, because the whole business of going beyond governments and operating directly on individuals can be traced back to Woodrow Wilson and the World War I concept of psychological operations without much heed of the consequences. We are nearly all liberals by temperament. We are nearly all, by temperament and perhaps by inherited ideology, even radicals. But we are all insufficiently sophisticated about the radical psychological and ideological effects of our manipulation of other people.

Let me turn then, as a final illustration of the role of psychological operations in international affairs, to the areas of foreign aid, technical assistance, and modernization. Since the Marshall Plan of 1948, and since the Point Four Program of 1949, the United States has been seeking to help other countries to modernize rapidly. It has been seeking to do this as much as possible by dealing directly with individuals in other countries. Some of the most telling popular criticism of our program has been that it does not really operate on the democratic model—that our aid goes to the elite and the governing few in these countries and that it never reaches the people. Americans are often terribly upset about this and feel that it is a bad thing. I'm not convinced that it is. I feel that the worst thing that could happen would be to give funds directly to the people who don't know what to do with foreign aid and aren't ready for changing their ways along channels that could be greased by our dollars.

Here is an area where we have been spending three to four billion dollars of the national budget each year—and quite a lot more than that if you consider the portion of the military budget which is spent for development purposes. Here is a kind of international relations which seems to be the psychologists' ideal of "peoples speaking to peoples." This is another one of those ideas which grow out of the democratic fallacy. There are no channels through which peoples speak to peoples. The channels of international communication always operate through government control, occasionally through some public corporation such as the BBC in Britain, and rarely through private corporations owning the mass media as in the United States. The American case is almost unique. Virtually no other country in the world leaves the ownership of these powerful media of communication in private hands. But even in these instances, the corporations do not represent "peoples speaking to peoples." There is always a gatekeeper, monitor, or censor. Perhaps it is well that it should be so. Peoples don't know what they want to say to other peoples.

The naive idea that it is good for a nation with a very high standard of living to communicate its own image to a nation with a very low standard of living—that "this lesson can pass as easily as ABC passes to a child in elementary school"—is a very dangerous assumption. I think on the contrary, that we are doing such pychological harm in the underdeveloped world that our childrens' children will pay some of the price for this. We have conveyed a picture of a better life, of the availability to all of the good things in life, and thereby helped to accelerate the desires (and demands) of peoples for these things. We have done this with the best will in the world.

I think that no nation has ever been more well-meaning than the American nation. But what we have done is to create a set of wants which cannot be satisfied within the lifetime of the people now living. We have helped to unbalance the ratio between the wants and the means to satisfy those wants by our insistence on operating directly and psychologically on individuals elsewhere in the world. This disruption of the want-get ratio—for people are taught by the mass media primarily to want—has gone so far that I don't think it is an exaggeration to say our psychological operations in recent years have been preparing a "revolution of rising frustrations." When people learn, as they must, that they cannot hope to get what they have been taught to want, there will follow a global accelera-tion of frustration with its attendant reaction-formations of aggres-sion and regression, neither of which is a state conducive to the modernization which American aid was intended to promote in the first instance.

Because American aid has been the principal source of develop-ment initiatives, American policy bears a heavy responsibility for the consequences. Because American practice has relied heavily on mass communication, Americans have a special responsibility for correcting the faulty psychological diagnosis on which this practice has been based. Because the faulty diagnosis has been drawn largely from untested assumptions and unwarranted inferences, largely by Americans, about the social psychology of American democracy, we have a particular responsibility for setting our sights straight.

To do this, we must bring more than amiable (and often aimless) good will to the role of psychology in international relations. We need to be better informed policy analysts and we need to be better disciplined psychological scientists. Only then will psychology begin to realize its significant potential as a contributor to the policy sciences of democratic development in the world political arena.

9

THE LANGUAGE
OF INTERNATIONAL
COMMUNICATION: SEMANTICS
AND LINGUISTICS

Harry Maynard
General Semantics Foundation
and
Time-Life International

I believe that the greatest roadblock to any form of human communication is what the social scientist refers to as ethnocentrism. The most observable differences between cultures are speech, dress, living habits, politics, and religion. But each culture is like a gigantic iceberg, carrying along beneath the surface of its observable differences its own assumptions, premises, and biases.

Language is the most pervasive, ubiquitous, and ethnocentric factor in our cultures. One can liken language to air—colorless, odorless, and necessary for survival; but language can also be lik-

137

ened to carbon monoxide, also colorless and odorless, but very poisonous.

Language acts as the cultural carrier of both the good and bad in our human predicament today. Language and symbols have given us the means for accumulation of knowledge and the tools to transmit it. Language has given expression to our finest ethical, philosophical, political, and legal insights. Language, in short, has given us civilizaton.

But too many people (and this includes some linguistic scholars) have examined language primarily as an artifact. In so doing, they remain prisoners of their ethnocentricity. Listen to Evelyn Waugh, scholar and writer of some repute, and his defense of the study of Greek and Latin as a necessity for anyone aspiring to write English:

I believe that the conventional defense of them is valid; that only by them can a boy fully understand that a sentence is a logical construction and that words *have basic inalienable meanings*, departure from which is either conscious metaphor or inexcusable vulgarity. Those who have not been so taught—most Americans and most women—unless they are guided by some rare genius, betray their deprivation. The old-fashioned test of an English sentence—will it translate?—still stands after we have lost the trick of translation.[1]

Why does he think this way? I think it is because during the eighteenth century the rise of the middle and upper middle classes took place in England. Their desire, like most middle class types, was to do the right thing. They had, like most middle class types, deep concern and apprehension about their language and saw in it a criterion of social prestige.

The semantic Emily Posts of that day naturally turned to classical Latin in order to frame a grammatical reverence for English. Many books on verbal etiquette appeared at the time, such as Bishop Lowth's *Short Introduction to English Grammar*, published in 1762. Thirty-three years later, in the United States, Lindley Murray wrote a grammar which sold a million copies between 1795 and 1850.

These are only a few of the many writers of that time who Latinized English and attempted to prescribe what was acceptable in speech and writing and what was not.

As a result, certain impressions sprang up that were both false and unfortunate:

1. Language is a divine institution, originally perfect, but debased by man. (No serious study of the history of language supports this idea; as a matter of fact, it demonstrates just the opposite.)

2. English is a corrupt and degenerate offspring of Greek and Latin. This canard is equally absurd. Yet a distinguished writer like Dryden did not credit English with having a grammar. He went so far as to carefully translate his words into Latin so that he could make corrections in his English. Supposedly, we still can't split infinitives in English or end a sentence with a preposition because it can't be done in Latin or gracefully translated into elegant Latin. Jonathan Swift felt so strongly about establishing the ground rules for "correct English" that he became one of the leading advocates for establishing an academy similar to the Spanish and French Academies. He did this because he felt it was the only way English could be protected from further corruption. Samuel Johnson, too, wrote his famous book on verbal etiquette with this aim in mind.

Recently, modern thinkers like Otto Jespersen, the Danish scholar, Bloomfield, and Sapir have clearly demolished this antiquated point of view. We see clearly today that language changes constantly and that change is inevitable and normal. Our spoken language is our language. Correctness rests on usage and usage is relative. Or, as some wit in the scientific world put it, "there are no absolutes, only relatives, and we have to get along with our relatives." This holds, too, with language.

Every man in every culture is immersed in an ocean of language. Like amphibians, we are part both of the world of words and of that of nonwords. This means we have all the accumulated wisdom and nonsense that language has helped construct wrapped up together in our individual psyches and personalities.

Our only hope of improving our culture and seeing through its accumulated nonsense as well as preserving its wisdom is to see through the verbal game—or we will suffer not only from a tyranny of words, but from the tyranny of nonsense assumptions and premises imbedded in the words and symbols of our culture.

Alfred Korzybski put it well:

We do not realize what tremendous power the structure of an habitual language has. It is not an exaggeration to say that it enslaves us through the mechanism of semantic reactions and that the structure which a language exhibits, and impresses upon us unconsciously, is *automatically projected* upon the world around us.[2]

How do we dig our way out of this predicament so that we can begin to communicate across our cultural barriers?

Aldous Huxley suggests:

A culture cannot be discriminatingly accepted, much less be modified, except by persons who have seen through it—by persons who have cut holes in the confining stockade of verbalized symbols and so are able to look at the world and, by reflection, at themselves in a new and relatively unprejudiced way. Such persons are not merely born; they must also be made. But how?

In the field of formal education, what the would-be hole-cutter needs is knowledge. Knowledge of the past and present history about the nature and limitations, the uses and abuses of language. A man who knows that there have been many cultures, and that each culture claims to be the best and truest of all, will find it hard to take too seriously the boastings and dogmatizings of his own tradition. Similarly, a man who knows how symbols are related to experience, and who practices the kind of linguistic self-control taught by the exponents of General Semantics, is unlikely to take too seriously the absurd or dangerous nonsense that, within every culture, passes for philosophy, practical wisdom and political argument.[3]

Note that Huxley writes of general semantics. How does this discipline differ from semantics? Historically, "semantics" has usually been associated with the narrow study of word meanings and the history of verbal etiquette. A semanticist of the classical variety can tell you that the largest French-speaking city in the world during the thirteenth century was—London. He can tell you that the word "giddy" once was used to describe a very bright and knowing young lady. He can trace the contraction "ain't" through increasingly less pejorative descriptions in successive editions of Webster's dictionary.

The general semanticist, however, is interested in the broader spectrum of human beings' responses to and uses of various symbols, including words. We humans also communicate by pictures, gestures, tone of voice, the clothes we wear, the automobiles we drive, and by many other devices with which we encode information and semaphore each other's nervous systems.

Scholars have classified over twenty different human senses. They are variations on the so-called "five windows of the soul." Thus, research in perceptual psychology shows that from two-thirds to 85 per cent of all the information the human nervous system takes in enters through the eye. Once we have taken in this information, we internalize it. We feed it back to ourselves. It shapes our idea of reality and eventually determines how we think, feel, and behave. This information becomes our assumptive knowledge.

The general semanticist is concerned with this process of sub-vocal talking to ourselves—the formation of our assumptions which we continuously apply to newly-internalized information. He recognizes that our languages contain our philosophies, and that each of our languages contains an implied theory of man and the universe. Korzybski and others see the parallel of language to cybernetics. They warn us that if you feed a lot of nonsense into a computer, you will receive a lot of nonsense in return. They urge us ever to be alert to the power of our assumptions.

The general semanticist tries to delimit our cultural biases and prejudices by inventing all sorts of specialized languages from calculus to symbolic logic, but even these get caught up in the strange grasp of assumptions. Our assumptive knowledge is so subtly acquired and internalized that it takes a great deal of special education and training to escape it, or as Huxley says, "cut through it."

Semantic rigidity was introduced formally into Western culture by Aristotelian logic, in which anything is either A or non-A. This is the law of the excluded middle, which I see is still with us today in the logic of Western movies, with their good guys and bad guys. In symbolic logic, however, a statement can be true, false, or indeterminate—or as they say in Scottish law, guilty, not guilty, or not proven. In the third case, we must go out and get more facts.

The force of Aristotelian logic, of semantic rigidities, of unconscious and erroneous assumptions is so great that our most creative and painstaking scientists are affected. Einstein said that the biggest roadblock he met in developing his theory of relativity was the notion that the sum of the angles of a triangle had to be 180 degrees. With this notion rigidly in place, he said, "I could not move ahead. I was creatively blocked." Once he got away from this assumption of Euclidean geometry, the way was open.

Let us look at another recent example. Scientists long suffered from the false assumption that it was beyond the reach of man to split the atom. Enrico Fermi did split the atom in 1934, at the University of Rome, but he did not know what he had done. Here is how the magazine, *Newsfront*, reports the experiment:

In January, 1934, Fermi received news that the famous husband and wife team of physicists, the Joliot-Curies, had discovered artificial radioactivity by bombarding aluminum with fast alpha particles. He decided to try the experiment himself, except that he used recently-discovered neutrons as projectiles.

Always a systematic man, he planned to test every one of the ninety-two elements starting with hydrogen. By summer Fermi reached element ninety-two, uranium. He discovered that the uranium became radioactive and at least one of the radioactive products was none of the existing elements close to uranium. Fermi decided he had discovered a new element with the atomic number 93, an element which does not exist on earth because it is too unstable.

For more than five years scientists repeated Fermi's uranium experiments thousands of times and came up with the same answer, *so great was the power of preconceived ideas.*

Had Fermi been aware that he had split the atom, possibilities of an atomic bomb would have been obvious back in 1934. *This could have given Hitler an arsenal with which to rule the world.*

After the war, *New York Times* reporter, William L. Lawrence asked Fermi how he had missed.

"It was a thin piece of aluminum foil, 3 mils thick, that stopped us all from seeing what actually took place," he answered.

In 1936, two Swiss physicists who were repeating Fermi's experiment left out the foil. The incredible reaction which followed caused them to agree "the damned instrument is sparking" and they hastily replaced the foil.[4]

When the greatest of our scientists are trapped by their culture, consider the predicament of us lesser mortals!

The biologist J. H. Woodger put it well. "Man makes metaphysics just as he breathes, without willing it and above all without doubting it most of the time."

What are the implications of the tyranny of our assumptions and our ethnocentric predicament for international communications today? Several years ago Frank Stanton, the president of CBS, pointed out that with the modern electronic devices we are now in the era of almost instantaneous communication; we are communicating in some instances close to the speed of light (186,000 miles a second in a perfect vacuum).

This means that our ethnocentric premises are bumping into each other at speeds unknown in the previous history of man. This goes a long way in explaining the turbulent state of the world today, with its tremendous clash between societies and cultures. With several countries having atomic weapons we are like scorpions in a bottle. Some of us have the potentiality of stinging each other and a good deal of the rest of mankind to death.

Previously, most human beings could sit on the sidelines when various individuals and groups quarreled over their short-term economic, political, and religious differences. This is no longer true. Cultural self-centeredness has always been a crime; now it threatens the survival of the majority of humanity.

What light can the student of semantics, general semantics, and linguistics throw on our human predicament? I believe general semantics can help us, as Wittgenstein has said, to "fight the bewitchment of our intellect by means of language." For only those who know what they deal with are free to deal with it. Language is one of our best tools for analyzing language. We have few others.

We must bring our assumed premises out into the open where they can be examined by ourselves and the world. Each of us has a perpetual self-inventory job to do in this area of premise evaluation. Each of us must also try to analyze the assumptions which underlie words and symbols in other cultures.

With the rapid development of communication media, man has released a force and accumulated energy that may be beyond his power to control. We must strive to master the media and that energy—thought energy—that is far more profound and exponential than atomic energy.

Our culture trains us and reinforces us to view the world through semantically-colored glasses. Language is our greatest habit. One of the notions of general semantics which is pretty well confirmed by modern psychology is that we all see the world, taste the world, smell the world, touch the world, hear the world differently. Out of necessity we all start with a different point of view. As Einstein put it, "The light that enters your eye is never the light that enters mine."

Perhaps the Far Eastern world has been most aware of how much our previous experiences color the information we take in. The Japanese film "Rashomon" made the fundamental point that there are great differences in individual evaluation of so-called "reality."

I am indebted to Walter Piston for the story of a prominent Chinese musician who, after hearing his first symphony concert, was asked which piece had pleased him most. He said he liked the first one best. His friend remarked that he showed excellent taste as it was Beethoven's "Leonora Overture." "No," replied the Chinese gentleman, "I mean the one before that—the piece they played before the conductor came on."

Our Western culture has begun to pay considerable attention to the specialized languages of science. As Wendell Johnson says, the most important part of science is the language of science.

However, we have strangely neglected the everyday language, our colloquial language, the language in which we do most of our thinking—the language with which we try to solve our moral, political, religious, and psychological problems. We dismiss these as a mere matter of semantics. We handle these problems as if they were below the attention of any deeply concerned person.

Let us remember that the limits of our world are sometimes determined by the limits of our language and symbol systems. Let us state our problems as well as we can. Necessity may be the mother of invention but definition is its father. We must recognize that the problems of man's inhumanity to man—problems of poverty, nutrition, living space, and disease—are before language. To state the problem properly is not the solution to the problem, but it may be a major step in solving it. And recognizing the assumptive differences built into our everyday languages may be one of the first steps in adjudicating our differences.

The scientifically oriented men in our society looking at our everyday language are in a unique historical position. We can master these new communication media. We do not have to accept our culture nor our language as fate, just as we soon won't have to accept the weather.

We can rise above our own vernaculars; we can transcend our own languages and, as Marshall McLuhan has pointed out, we can transcend "the limitations of our own assumptions by a critique of them." He continues:

We can now live, not just amphibiously in divided and distinguished worlds, but pluralistically in many worlds and in many media and languages. We are no more committed to one culture—to a single ratio among the human senses—any more than to one book or to one language or to one technology. Our need today is, culturally, the same as the scientist's who seeks to become aware of the bias of the instruments of research in order to correct that bias.[5]

If we do adopt this attitude toward both our cultures and our languages, we can then perhaps begin to better settle our international differences.

10

INTERNATIONAL NEWS MEDIA

Robert Manning
Editor, *The Atlantic Monthly*

The American press over-all—that is, including television and radio journalism—shares several characteristics that are directly relevant to its role in providing information *about*, and its tendency to affect the conduct *of*, foreign affairs. Briefly:

(1) It is fascinated with speed and "exclusivity," frequently to the exclusion of quality, although tending more and more to a stronger interest in analysis and interpretation.

(2) It is insistent on its economic viability, including the right to make profits.

(3) It is extremely vocal about its rights and prerogatives, but it

suffers from what might be called "professional laryngitis" when the discussion turns to its public responsibilities. It is of many minds on the question of its obligations, if any.

(4) Because of the great advances in technology and the shrinkage of the world into one in which a grenade explosion in Saigon or a coup in Accra has direct meaning to a household in Iowa, the press is in danger of being overwhelmed by the very torrent of events, facts, and opinions that constantly pours in on it.

(5) It is convinced that its primary enterprise is that of disclosure.

All of these characteristics are pertinent to our discussion, but the last three are most important, for it is in these three characteristics that we find the differences of interest, of objective, and of purpose that separate American journalism from American government.

One day in 1851 in Great Britain, Lord Derby was provoked by a story in the *Times* of London to the point of complaining that if the press aspired to share the influence of statesmen, it must also share in the responsibilities of statesmen. The *Times* next day printed a classic answer: "The first duty of the press," it said, "is to obtain the earliest and most correct intelligence of the events of the time and instantly, by disclosure of them, to make them the common property of the nation. The press lives by disclosure." The editorial went on: "The statesman's duty is precisely the reverse. He cautiously guards from the public eye the information by which his actions and opinions are regulated. He reserves his judgment of passing events until the latest moment and then he records it in obscure or conventional language. He strictly confines himself, if he be wise, to the practical interests of his country or to those turning immediately upon it."

A public official in this country is not permitted to take so luxurious a view, and to assert a right to tell only what he pleases, and only at moments he finds convenient. Indeed, many journalists, and some other members of the public in this country, take the position that a government official is subject to provide *on demand* public disclosure and explanations of any policies and affairs that bear on the public interest. The conflict between government and journalism on this score is one of the most demanding dilemmas in the conduct of our business as a nation.

On many of the most serious and most sensitive questions of foreign affairs today, press and government diverge in their purposes and in their obligations. Neither government nor journalism has given this divergence the searching, honest scrutiny it requires. I see no magic formula by which the built-in conflict can ever be resolved, but it ought at least to be possible for officials and journalists to arrive at a clearer understanding of the problem and of how it bears on their interest. Too often, scrutiny of this matter is left to the press alone, so discussion falls quickly into the dust-heap of clichés and self-righteous laments. Truer even than the maxim that war is too important to be left to the generals is the fact that freedom of the press is too important a right in this country to be left only to the publishers, editors, broadcasters, and reporters.

It is helpful to read the phrase "freedom of the press" in the full context of the First Amendment, because the more superficial spokesmen for journalism (and these seem characteristically to include the most vocal) often imply that freedom of the press is an economic or business right when in fact it is a human right. They seem often to be saying that press and public are always synonymous and that the press is therefore the *sole* custodian of "the people's right to know," when in fact, the press is merely the principal conduit of that right. I should add, in fairness, that there are times when *only* the press appears to care enough to shout about it, and we should be grateful for that.

One could talk at length about the press's shortcomings in its exercise of its role as principal nourisher of the right to know. Our journalism today has many faults—sloppiness, omission, small and middle scale venality, some notable cases of ballooning ego, and, as I mentioned earlier, a general lack of agreed ethics. But the bigger problems lie in the almost daily instances of tension or conflict between one essential of our generally democratic system, the free press, and certain other essentials of the system. For example, in the current argument about "the right to know" versus "the right to a fair trial" we have conflict between two constitutional rights. There is almost equal weight in both rights and, while a formal solution eludes both press and bar, these equal pressures induce serious efforts to cope with the conflict.

The conflict as it affects foreign affairs is far less clear-cut, far more elusive. I refer to the dilemma faced by a country like ours, an open society reliant upon open discussion and broad consent, as it tries to conduct foreign policy in a world of many different systems, a world of many enemies, a world in which others have advantages of the tools of censorship, suppression, secrecy, and deceit.

Anyone concerned with the conduct of foreign policy must come to some working conclusions about the "responsibilities" or "obligations" of the press, as against its prerogatives, and about the ability of the press to convey with coherence the vast flow of information available to it. On the matter of its responsibilities, we find journalism itself in considerable disarray, and some of its spokesmen themselves flagrantly inconsistent.

Does the press owe allegiance to a country? Or to the ideals of disclosure and truth? This question frequently bedevils an editor or publisher in a practical way. One assumes it bedeviled Colonel McCormack when his paper broke the story of our breaking of the Japanese code early in World War II. We know it occurred for editors of the *New York Times*, and caused them to underplay on the eve of the Bay of Pigs a story on American-led preparation for invasion. And we know that some of those same editors have since wondered whether in serving the U.S. government in that instance, they really served truth and the United States and the public as well.

(It is interesting to speculate briefly on this. If the *Times* had published advance details of the Bay of Pigs plan, might it have torpedoed the undertaking? If there had been no Bay of Pigs, would Khrushchev have made a solider reading of the young President Kennedy and later decided against placing Soviet missiles in Cuba? If there had been no Cuban missile crisis, where might Khrushchev be today, or relations between Moscow and Peking? If there had been no Bay of Pigs and no missile crisis, is it possible that the mind of one Lee Harvey Oswald might have fastened on some entirely different fixation in some entirely different place on some day other than November 22, 1963? A fantastic and highly improbable web of speculation? I wonder.)

The flag is waved and the incantations of patriotism are loudly sounded at every annual meeting of the American Newspaper Publishers Association and American Society of Newspaper Editors, and I dare say that most of their members would say with Carl Schurz, "Our country, right or wrong," or would share the sentiments of Andrew Tully, a Washington correspondent who once wrote, "No self-respecting newsman would deliberately print something harmful to his government." These sentiments, of course, would have the emphatic approval of any official concerned with American policies, from the President down to the Class Three Foreign Service officer trying to negotiate a cocoa agreement with the new Ghanaian government. But they are not shared by all journalists, and for good reason. A press that is not free to disclose even at the expense of its own country or its own security is not altogether free. Says Alan Barth of the *Washington Post*: "A press

which enjoys such independence of government is almost bound
to be, by definition, in some degree irresponsible . . . . our country
right or wrong is a dangerous sort of sentimentality for individuals;
for newspapers it represents a total abdication of responsibility.
For the responsibility of a newspaper is not to governments; it is
to values, to ideas, to human beings."

In reality, there are few American journalists who would apply
Barth's dictum to the ultimate if they believed that disclosure might
seriously harm Americans or an American policy. Indeed, his own
newspaper occasionally kills or neglects stories on request from
the White House or other high places. But I think the best men in
journalism would side with Barth, and it is important that any
government official who deals with, or tries to understand, the
operations and functions of American journalism realize that at a
given moment of crisis or development in international politics, the
good journalist's loyalty need not and may not be directed at the
same objective as the government's. (I speak of government in the
ideal sense—that is, of officials whose interest in nondisclosure is in
collision with journalism's interest in disclosure for sound reasons
of public interest rather than from a desire to cover up error or
deceive the public. Those in government who fudge and manipu-
late in order to serve personal ends or obscure their failings deserve
all the fire that can be directed against them; the difficulty comes
when it is hard to find the line between what may be public-
serving and what self-serving in an official's decision to be obscure,
to withhold, or to postpone a revelation.) But there are bound to
be occasions every day in the complex field of international politics
when a government official may as validly decide to withhold
information in the interest of serving the public (that is, by helping
a public policy to succeed), as a journalist may validly decide that
the public shall get facts even though their disclosure might benefit

an antagonist or betray prematurely an American negotiating position.

The difficulty with the process is that the presumed beneficiaries of such arbitrary judgment-making, the American public, get no chance to arbitrate because they do not know until after publication, or after discovery of a suppression, whether they prefer to take the consequences of knowing—and have the rest of the world know—or of not knowing. Later I will try to illustrate the kinds of information about which such doubts may arise.

What the intelligent members of the press will and will not tolerate in government information handling depends in great part on a mixture of large imponderables and personal whims. During and after the Cuban missile crisis, for example, the *New York Times'* Arthur Krock rose up in wrath and hurled a mighty thunderbolt at President Kennedy and his Administration for the alleged "managing of the news" of that crisis, even though most journalists seem to have accepted that the secrecy of the U.S. deliberations and decisions between the discovery of the Soviet missiles on October 16 and the President's speech on the night of October 22 was vital to the success of the U.S. response to Moscow. Still Krock was critical. Yet when a President he more strongly admired was busily sliding several peas beneath walnut shells to mount the Johnson peace offensive, Mr. Krock wrote in the *New York Times*: "The secrecy in which the Administration has enveloped its current search for suspension of the war in Vietnam is essential to the purpose. . . . *The people's right to know must, at times, be limited in the national interest.*"

Walter Lippmann, watching from England the Dominican crisis of 1965, sharply indicted the government's handling of information (and misinformation) in that crisis while warmly applauding the performance of American correspondents on the scene—a performance that was, in my estimation, perhaps as bad as the Administration's. Yet later he joined Mr. Krock in saying: "If anything useful is to come of it all, the governments concerned in the Vietnam war are right in keeping secret whatever diplomatic action may now be taking place."

I cite these two distinguished journalists not to attack them, nor even to charge them with inconsistency, but to illustrate that even within the profession most directly concerned with the flow of information, there is implicit recognition that the public interest can sometimes be harmed by disclosure. Mr. Lippmann, in fact, goes much further. He accepts as fact, as he wrote in 1941, that "obviously the President and the Administration officials and the Congressmen in touch with them have the means for informing themselves on the realities of the labor situation and the defense program and of the war that no one else, not even the most conscientious newspaper reporters, can possess."

"The notion that public opinion can and will decide all issues," Lippmann has written, "is in appearance very democratic. In practice it undermines and destroys democratic government. For when everyone is supposed to have a judgment about everything nobody in fact is going to know much about anything. . . . The only effect of inviting everybody to judge every public question is to confuse everybody about everything. . . ."

It seems to me that this suggests one of the great negative powers of the combined government and press today—the power to confuse. This brings us to the part of the problem that, in my estimation, towers over secrecy and suppression in seriousness. Unquestionably there are times when the government arrogates to itself certain interludes of secrecy, or privacy, in which to ponder solutions or negotiate settlements with other governments. Undeniably there are occasions when the conflict between the public's right to know and the government's determination to make a policy succeed is settled on the government's terms. Press and public find out later what has occurred. It is true, too, that officials on occasion decide arbitrarily what shall be said or not be said about a given situation at the time it is developing—although no more arbitrarily, of course, than the news editor who decides what stories to throw away or to bury back in the want ads of his newspaper, or the broadcaster who decides which five minutes' worth to use of the previous twenty-four hours' accumulation of news. These arbitrary invasions of the public's right to know do happen, because even a democratic government finds itself believing in Heisenberg's principle of uncertainty in nuclear physics as it applies to the process of foreign affairs; to wit, it is usually not possible to describe a diplomatic situation publicly, however accurately, without changing it and making it different; the public comment becomes part of the situation.

This happens as a matter of course. Diplomatic correspondents are fascinated about what is *going* to happen in an interesting situation and they frequently pursue this at the expense of reporting fully and usefully what *has* happened. I know of top-rank correspondents in Washington who have spent literally dozens of man-hours trying to learn before their competitors the next likely ambassador to an important capital. So diligently is this ferreting-out game pursued that, with a man of Lyndon Johnson's fierce irritability at being preguessed, an almost sure-fire way of sinking a man in Washington has been to leak his prospective appointment to an important job.

In Geneva a few years ago, intensive reporting by a couple of American correspondents dug out essential details of an imminent U.S. proposal in the disarmament negotiations and went so far as to reveal not only the government's position but its fallback position.

Naturally that meant the presentation had to be changed in order to trim back some of the advantage that this disclosure handed to the Russian delegation.

In 1962 there developed a most interesting illustration of the problem that can be raised by the perfectly valid application of journalism's desire to disclose a project which requires privacy in preparation if it is to succeed. Interestingly enough, the project was an exercise in public diplomacy. It was decided by some military and diplomatic officials in Washington that American interests might be served if some of the neutralists in important countries like India and Indonesia were shown the speed with which the United States could bring power to their defense in the event either was attacked (as not much later India was, by Red Chinese forces). The proposal was to send units of the nuclear-armed Sixth Fleet on a goodwill cruise into the Indian Ocean. The first necessity was to get advance permission from Indian and Indonesian government officials for calls at their ports. The discussions had barely begun when a reporter got wind of the story and, by publishing it, gave anti-American elements in both countries time in which to stir up loud demonstrations against the projected "nuclear invasion." This ended the matter. It is worthless to argue whether the story should have been written (it was legitimate journalism, and it conveyed no "secret" in the practical sense; indeed, one could argue that persons in the United States who might dislike this sort of nuclear diplomacy deserved the right to know about it in time to resist it.) Anyway, here was a good case of Heisenberg's principle proving out in foreign affairs.

A noteworthy case was the Skybolt affair of 1962. Certain Pentagon and army officials who had an interest in keeping the Skybolt missile leaked the word that it was to be dropped from our weapons arsenal by Secretary of Defense McNamara. This set off a crisis in Anglo-American relations. The British had been counting on the missile to extend the life of their nuclear deterrent and the premature release deprived American and British officials of time in which to prepare alternatives and to enable the British government to plan its own public handling of the question. This crisis in turn led to the ill-prepared and diplomatically costly Nassau conference between President Kennedy and Prime Minister Macmillan. I would not try to make a case that there would have been no serious repercussions otherwise, for there would have been. Nor would I try to maintain that had it not been for the Nassau decisions, General de Gaulle would not have then moved to block Britain from the Common Market and launch his fight to push American influence back from the Continent. He was going to do that anyway, but there is no question that the Skybolt fiasco gave him impetus and excuse for proceeding when and as he did and probably furthered that process.

None of these examples—and in day-to-day matters of diplomacy and negotiation such incidences are legion—involves anything like the transmitting of important secrets to the enemy; in fact they all happened in the normal process of journalism. I raise them merely to illustrate that journalism involves constant intrusions on diplomacy and has a direct effect on the public interest. I would be interested in knowing, for example, whether the public, in defense of whose "right to know" the press printed the advance tip on the Sixth Fleet maneuver, or Skybolt, or the United States fallback position at Geneva might have preferred to let the negotiations proceed and learn about them later. But how is one to measure this?

The fact is, however, that in the shaping and execution of important American foreign policies today, only a small fraction of essential information is secret, and the disclosure of those secrets is inevitable if not imminent. As for distortion or peddling of harmful partial truth, he is a rare official who succeeds more than once in seriously misleading the wiser and more persistent of that tough-minded pack, the Hounds of Gutenberg. In fact, if the newsmen were as competent at passing on the available facts in sufficient quantity and with coherence as they are at smoking out trends and sniffing out the bogus, our journalists would be very good indeed.

For it is not the availability of information or access to officials that is the major problem, no matter how many Moss Committee reports or publishers' ringing denunciations you read. The problem relates to our ability—government, press, and public at large—to collect and find a certain useful coherence out of the flood of information that is available.

I spoke of journalism's difficulty in coping with the torrent. We all know that far more pertinent information on matters of direct consequence to each of us and our families is spread out before us each hour, day, and week than we can possibly scan, let alone assimilate. This is true, too, for all the media, for as events proliferate, so do the means of communicating them. "Our present news situation in the United States," the late A. J. Liebling once wrote, "is breaking down to something like the system of water distribution in the Casbah, where peddlars wander about with goatskins of water on small donkeys, and the inhabitants send down an oil tin and a couple of pennies when they feel thirsty." The more they thirst, the more oil cans and the more peddlars appear on the scene. Yet the drinks remain the same few pennies' worth at a time. The newspapers thrive more than ever because radio and TV titillate with small bits of news and make us thirsty for more detail. The news magazines thrive, often by dressing up what the newspapers have already said with spicy verbs and aromatic adjectives, because the daily and Sunday press are found inadequate. Yet while the newsweeklies reach for more and more millions of subscribers, the fortnightlies and monthlies go up in circulation too, because all that precedes them is assumed—correctly—to be not sufficient to slake the thirst. In addition, more than 1,500 newsletters, some of them costing hundreds of dollars a year, are prospering because hundreds of thousands believe they are not getting enough of the pertinent facts from the other publications they read. Add to this the explosion of "book journalism" in recent years—a phenomenon which, after millions upon millions of words were written and spoken during the 1960 and 1964 presidential campaigns, could nonetheless make tremendous best-sellers of Theodore White's months-after-the-fact books on *The Making of the President*. Or which, while my associates and I were wondering eight days after the great power blackout of 1965 what our monthly magazine might say about it a few weeks later, could deposit on my desk a full-fledged book dealing with the event.

One would think that this tremendous profusion of the means of communication and of the techniques, venturesomeness, and purposes of the communicators would have helped to enhance our understanding of what is going on in the world and how it all relates to us; that it would have helped to simplify our ways of arriving at a reasonable public consensus as to American policies and actions in the world. What has it achieved?

For the public, it has added an immense number of new voices, of new opinions, of new sources of fact, and a considerable sprinkling of fancy, but it has not brought with it any great increase in the amount of time which the average busy citizen can allot to reading and studying what is available. It is a development that has favored the more emphatic, more arbitrary, and more opinionated purveyors of information; and it too often has favored the more shrill. Even the most studious follower of affairs finds himself on occasion relieved to reach through the welter to the columnist, commentator, or anonymous headline or news magazine analysis that seems to say with Alsopian certainty: "Forget the rest of them, my good man. This is how it is."

For the communicator, the profusion has increased the strains and

risks that go with competition and presented him with the choice
of tremendously expanding his own resources, or relying increasingly on wire services, syndicates, pooled efforts, or not-altogether-
known sources of distant supply. As the vast increase in demand
and in available information has flooded in on newspaper and news
agencies, they have done very little to adapt new methods of news
presentation and appallingly little to raise personnel standards or
improve professional training. In newspapers, substantially the
same mechanics, the same approaches to news handling and com-
position of news pages are still in use in these days when we are
engaged in fifteen to twenty crises at a time, as in prewar days,
when we were likely to be involved in one or two. The requirements for admission to almost any profession have changed considerably in recent years, but a man need not show a great deal
more today to break into journalism than he had to demonstrate
in the days when Hildy Johnson was filing for *The Front Page*.

Anyone who cares to see the physical problem of riding the
information torrent need only visit a radio station or a newspaper
office on a normal day. He will see, for example, that the main
Associated Press news ticker in one day usually carries about 27,000
words, or twenty-seven newspaper columns, of foreign affairs
news. Yet when he looks at a typical newspaper he will find that
all but about 25 per cent of that material has been thrown away,
that as little as 3 to 8 per cent of the paper's space is devoted that
day to foreign affairs. Mightily the news editors and deskmen try
to stay afloat in the flood. They cut, they blue pencil. They encompass a dozen complexities into one brief, black headline. They
consign one item to the bright exposure of page one, another to the
limbo of the back page. And at a tremendous rate, they omit.
What to throw away? That is, alas, one of the most demanding
problems today's editor confronts.

Every day journalism exercises swiftly, sometimes precisely, sometimes with bias, sometimes without, almost always arbitrarily, the act of judgment. Every front page is an announcement of the editor's judgment, a daily symbol of his effectiveness as a manager of the news. Every newspaper and magazine is a transitory monument to the judgment of its editors and owners. NBC's Fulbright hearings are CBS' "I Love Lucy" reruns. It is the daily judgment of editors of the *Washington Post* that its readers need or want approximately five pages of comic strips; it is the judgment of editors of the *New York Times* that its readers do not need or want any. *Time* magazine's George Kennan is unrecognizable as the George Kennan of the *New Republic*. It was the judgment of *Time's* press section that the young newsmen who helped bring down the Diem regime were prejudiced incompetents; of *Newsweek's* press section that they were intrepid saints deserving of mass canonization and the Pulitzer prize. Where Lippmann sees the threat of Armageddon, Alsop sights a peace threat.

From the readers' standpoint, this great proliferation of opinion, speculation, and even of *versions* of the facts ought to have created for the media a credibility problem that is oddly akin to the credibility problem journalism keeps attributing (properly, I would add) to the government. The more one knows of the difficulty of choosing what to print and what to throw away, the more he will wonder what he can or should believe or, to put it another way, what and how much is missing from what he is being told to believe.

I have talked more about the press than about government for the good reason that the proportion is usually the other way around; the shortcomings and errors of government are fair game for the press and are constantly under scrutiny and discussion. In fact, the Supreme Court has stipulated that a public official may be libeled with impunity if that seems to serve a reasonably useful purpose. On the other hand, the press is, as I said, remarkably taciturn about its own shortcomings and errors. I don't mean to suggest that my government experience has left me feeling that Washington pays sufficient respect or applies sufficient imagination to the problem of communicating with the public. While too many journalists know too little about the way government really works and the way decisions really are made, an appalling number of government officials are woefully ignorant of how the press works, or what its standards and its needs are. The President's tendency to believe that the press ought to print only what *he* wants to read is well known and, while discomfiting, is perhaps understandable in a man who occupies such high loneliness and who is as single-minded as this President. President Kennedy was not much better on that score; President Eisenhower would not have been if he had been much of a reader; Presidents Truman and Roosevelt were pretty shortsighted about it too—although they seemed to be able to laugh a little more. What is disturbing, however, is to see how far down the syndrome reaches among men of high intelligence and high responsibility who ought to know better about the process and have a greater respect for it.

Secondly, Washington officials read astonishingly little of what is printed except that dealing directly with their august affairs, pausing perhaps to catch fragments on the "Today" show while shaving, to digest a couple of front pages and their favorite (or most irritating) columnist and perhaps a *Times* editorial before midday, and otherwise relying on aides to call to their attention longer articles of moment, or to some of the more reflective journals when they happen to have an article that deals with an issue of particular interest. The fact is that life at the top in Washington is so brutal in its demands on officials that they dole their time and concentration like ambergris, favoring frequently what they most want to read rather than what perhaps they should. The rest they take in capsule digests prepared by underlings; this applies even to much of the official cable traffic, which in the State Department today can mount to as much as 10,000 incoming and outgoing messages a day.

Thirdly, officials are apt to think of the communications media as some sort of monolith, and even while they think of a few Washington personalities as individuals—by-line correspondents, bureau chiefs, and the pundits—they seem to consider them in group as a monolith's all-powerful Politburo. They find themselves speaking more and more to the minds and reflexes of a few. Even the speeches prepared by top foreign policy officials for delivery in the further reaches of the United States are really written for Washington news consumption, and I know many officials who feel abused if the story is written by some fellow in San Francisco or Des Moines "who just doesn't have the background for this sort of thing." A speech, one assumes, is supposed to communicate with the people it is delivered to, but in foreign affairs that may be its very least purpose.

Fourthly, though there has been, I believe, a considerable up-grading of what used to be called "the information function," it is still common for officials to think reflexively of the press as "the hostiles" and to associate their own information officials with the other side. President Kennedy did more than any predecessor to bring his information people into the middle of affairs, thereby giving them the first-hand opportunity to observe the nature of a problem and providing them with an authoritativeness that made them acceptable to newsmen as first-rank sources. Generally speaking, however, the tendency still is for officials to think of the public affairs man as being somehow "outside of policy" and to deal with him as a sort of Western Union boy, to be tricked out in a visored cap and sent off to deliver night letters. Professional newsmen will always feel a need to go around and above such officials, until they find "someone who is in on the show."

This downgrading of information to a subsidiary function can be very consequential. In nuclear diplomacy every move made can be more important for the public reaction it sets off than for the actual machinery of government which is engaged. When President Kennedy decided something had to be done about the balance of payments problem, he turned to the Pentagon, the biggest spender of money overseas. With his usual efficiency, Secretary McNamara figured he could save so many millions of dollars in gold drain by doing X, Y, and Z. X and Y were all right, but Z involved a serious cut in U.S. military forces in Europe. (This at a time when de Gaulle had begun an all-out attack on the credibility of the American commitment to defend Europe. This at a time when Berlin was still an issue and any pullback of forces could inflame that city again. This at a time when the Germans were extra-nervous.) Almost immediately, any official who had to deal with NATO—including those who had been inclined to disdain the information function—perceived the danger. The effect on public opinion had become the determining factor in the political-economic decision.

Fifthly, the government's allocation of resources to the public discussion and understanding of foreign affairs within the United States is self-defeatingly low. I am aware that the reluctance of Congress to spend more on the overseas program, the USIA, is in itself shortsighted; we ought to be able to put more into the information and propaganda program of a world we want to influence than about the cost of one Polaris submarine. But by comparison, the home front situation is ludicrous. As a matter of idle curiosity, I spent considerable time when I was in government trying to arrive at an honest figure of the money appropriated for public affairs activities in the Pentagon and the armed forces. I might as well have been wearing a Cossack hat, smelling of vodka, strumming a balalaika, and trying to gain admittance to the Los Alamos testing grounds in early 1945. The figures are neatly obscured in the over-all Pentagon budget, but I think a figure of some $35,000,000 is probably on the low side and it may be as high as $50,000,000 a year. For the Department of State, the budget for the Bureau of Public Affairs in the current fiscal year is about $1,600,000 and almost a third of that provides for the forty-one personnel in the Office of History and its printing of volumes of documents twenty and more years old. In my last year in the Department, we succeeded for the first time in getting an allocation of $28,000 to let the Department of State become the last of perhaps fifty government departments and agencies to make use of the film medium as a means of spreading information about foreign affairs. I cannot hazard a guess as to the number of personnel who handle the multitude of public relations functions for the Pentagon, but it runs into the several thousands without even counting military public information officers overseas. Public affairs personnel in the Department of State number approximately 150 today, plus fifteen public affairs advisors sprinkled among the Department's regional bureaus.

As with the USIA, the problem is Congressional. Not a great increase in personnel or funds would be necessary to bring the Department's program up to reasonable performance, but this is one of the most sensitive issues in Congress. Few of its members, even those whose party is in power, like the idea of voting funds to a Department for activities that could equip it to go out to the country and campaign for the very foreign programs or commitments the Congressman might be against. It may be that a substantial increase in funds is *not* the best way; I am not sure. It may be that the increased public interest in foreign affairs and the increased desire for first-hand knowledge about it can induce greater efforts within journalism and within the public service organizations and foundations to bring foreign policy officials and the public into greater contact. That would certainly be an acceptable substitute, and perhaps a healthier one than an increase in government spending for the program. But I would also like to see a considerable cutback at the same time in the amounts that the military can throw about for public affairs purposes.

I am aware that this recital has been more the presentation of a building inspector than that of an architect. That is deliberate. I do not think the problems I have been discussing lend themselves to easy solutions or orderly compartmentalizing. A great deal of it can be classified under the legend: "That's the way it works." It is surprising, when you see all the baling wire and improvisation and wrong-guessing and bullheadedness that goes into it, that it works as well as it does, and in almost every crucial moment or boiling crisis you can sense ways in which the process could go suddenly, seriously wrong. If I were to press for one way of decreasing the chances of that happening, it would be to urge serious thinking about some sort of plan to bring the functions of government and of communication into closer understanding of each other, without trying to end what I believe to be an absolutely essential conflict of interest. Every official who achieves a position of decision-influencing importance in government—and this can go down fairly deeply into the ranks of a place like the Department of State—ought to be required to familiarize himself with both the operations and the litanies of journalism; the Foreign Service could well consider the idea of arranging for promising officers to serve a two or three year tour in some journalistic function outside government; a diplomat these days isn't worth much if he can't write, and the worst that could happen would be a sharpening of his prose style. Journalism, on the other hand, ought to be encouraged, even provoked, into abandoning its reflex about newsmen who go into political or government jobs. The reflex is changing, but there is still a substantial hangover of the old-fashioned notion that once a man has gone into a public job he has burned the bridges of so-called objectivity behind him. This is nonsense. A reporter or news editor who spent two or three years in a responsible government job (and I do not by any means think that it should be confined to an information job; on the contrary, other assignments would be more valuable for him and produce more of value for the government) ought to be immensely more valuable as an interpreter and communicator of complicated events, and a far better judge of when a journalist ought to cooperate with or contend with his government. This in itself would be a great step toward making the most of democracy's great paradox.

II

COMMUNICATIONS TO OPEN AND CLOSED SOCIETIES

Howland H. Sargeant
Radio Liberty Committee

Within the context of the Edward R. Murrow Center's concept of public diplomacy I shall examine two problems of communication. First, our attempts to make other peoples in the open societies of the world understand what we Americans are up to. Second, the quite different problem of trying to do the same thing with the peoples who now live within a closed or semiclosed society—roughly one-third of the inhabitants of the earth.

Although I shall refer to each of the major ways in which a nation seeks to achieve its foreign policy goals—through deals, goods, force, and ideas—most of what I have to say relates to the symbols with which a nation clothes its policies and actions. By themselves, ideas used as an instrument of national policy can accomplish little, but used in concert with diplomatic, economic, and military programs, they can make our public diplomacy conspicuously successful. Witness a military undertaking such as the Berlin airlift, or the commitment of American troops to Europe or to the United Nations forces in Korea; a program like the Marshall Plan in the economic field; a statement of policy like the Truman Doctrine, or President Eisenhower's appeal for "a true and total peace," or President Kennedy's American University speech calling for a re-examination of our attitudes toward the Soviet Union and the cold war; the development through diplomacy of NATO, and the even more difficult task of holding it together.

Public Diplomacy to Open Societies

The dialogue between Americans and open societies differs profoundly in character, content, and diversity from that in which we can engage with closed societies. In a democracy like ours the government and its official actions will seldom produce more than a fraction—perhaps only 5 or 10 per cent—of the impact Americans make on other peoples in open societies. This should not be misinterpreted. The United States Information Agency and our officially supported cultural relations programs are performing absolutely essential jobs. At an annual cost of a little over $200 million—about half the amount our three leading soap detergent companies spend in their advertising and sales promotion campaigns in a year—these official programs are contributing in major ways to the realization of United States objectives. Having said this, however, I should make it crystal clear that I do not believe a democracy's programs of official communication can *manipulate* other peoples' attitudes and behavior. On the contrary, I contend that cultural relations, in the broadest sense, are a stronger tool for international relations than diplomacy, in the limited meaning of that word, and information programs are merely a tool of cultural relations. A few countries in the world have understood this. The French were the first and they built their foreign relations on this premise as early as 1860. I am not sure that our country has yet understood that cultural relations are the strongest arm of diplomacy.

The government's official information program can help enormously in attaching the meaning that we want accepted to a particular action or policy decision. But in the long run I am convinced that the impact of the private American on foreign public opinion in the open societies is considerably greater than that of official communication. The behavior and actions of the American government and the American people themselves, with all their contradictions and diversity, create the image that other peoples living in open societies see. Skillful propagandists can to some extent influence this unintended and unplanned image, but the true picture cannot be concealed for long.

Consider that the American commercial motion picture plays to about 75 million admissions each week outside the United States. American books, newspapers, and magazines reach millions of foreign readers. American television productions are seen more and more on screens abroad. There are overseas more than a million American military personnel and nearly 300,000 civilian employees of the military services and their dependents. Another 640,000 Americans are resident abroad, including employees of American business and of civilian government departments. In a recent year, well over two million Americans traveled abroad (excluding Canada and Mexico) and nearly a million foreign travelers entered the United States.

There are more than 35,000 representatives of American business working overseas. In a recent year, 2,500 American companies were operating 7,000 branches abroad. Alfred North Whitehead was probably correct in selecting commerce as "the great example of intercourse in the way of persuasion."

These private Americans in face-to-face meetings, in business relationships, and in their products and mass media, have a powerful, and often unpredictable, impact on foreign public opinion and attitudes. Whether they persuade wisely or foolishly, create confidence or mistrust, it is nevertheless in those private channels that the broad tides of persuasion really flow. Our pluralistic society with its contradictions creates a confusing view when seen from abroad and there is little resemblance between America and Sir William Hayter's description of a closed society like the U.S.S.R. where "every public action in their own country can be made if desired to conform to their diplomatic needs."

American official communication that is intended to affect foreign attitudes in open societies must proceed against a background of kaleidoscopic, contradictory, and confusing private American communication that does *not* have any such political purpose. Our official communication, however, can enjoy the advantages of having objectives that most foreign peoples hold in common with us and of being based on truth and therefore of promising no more than we can perform. Further, we have increasing opportunity to know what public attitudes in foreign open societies are. Other chapters in this book describe the growing importance of public opinion polls in guiding us correctly. The work of psychologists is giving us a better understanding of the reality worlds of the people we wish to communicate with. We can seek the cooperation of nationals of the country in evaluating the impact of broadcasts, magazines, books, or motion pictures, or, indeed, we can even pre-test materials designed for mass media there. There are citizens in some open societies who genuinely believe it important in this interdependent world to assist us Americans in making our way of life, problems, and purposes known to their fellow countrymen. And some wise Americans believe that in each country where we carry on a persuasion program of our own we should try to help develop a reciprocal flow of information *toward* the United States. Such a concept of mutual understanding might lead to less emphasis on Americans conducting persuasion on foreign soil and to more emphasis on a partnership arrangement between Americans and others for the mutual welfare of both. This could help redress the imbalance that exists between us and even our closest neighbors. The American Assembly concluded in 1964:

> The fact that the vast majority of Americans are still virtually unaware of the crisis which has arisen in the relations of English and French Canada contrasts sharply with the information available to all Canadians on a daily, even hourly basis concerning the struggle in America to provide equal opportunity for our Negro citizens.[1]

In summary, from the open societies we can find out a great deal about the assumptions on which people are basing their current attitudes and opinions. We can learn a great deal about their values, hopes, fears, and expectations. Even so, we will still occasionally seem to bungle and confuse even in our official communication. Our Vietnam policy has not been clearly understood abroad, nor indeed at home, and it has puzzled many in other open societies with its apparent conflicts, such as enlisting the United Nations to bring about a cease-fire, but at the same time continuing the bombing of North Vietnam.

Even in open societies there are going to be times when we are proven incapable of judging in advance of the event what action may flow from a given set of attitudes and assumptions and what may trigger it. Our attempt after the India-China border war in 1962 to give India a megawatt transmitter which Nehru wanted badly to contest Peking's radio propaganda in Southeast Asia touched off an uproar because the Voice of America wanted to use the transmitter three hours daily for broadcasts to China. The Soviet Union finally supplied the transmitter through a five-year interest-bearing loan with no strings attached. Later we saw what Lloyd Free called "more extreme manifestations of public action in the form of demonstrations, picketing and rioting" overturning the foreign policy of Indonesia in a stunning and unpredicted display of the power of deeply held although not visibly demonstrated convictions.

Public Diplomacy as Applied to a Closed Society

In a closed society, those in power invariably try to limit the ideas and information reaching their citizens from outside, and to pass as much of this outside information through distorting prisms as they believe will suit their purposes.

How do you actually influence directly or indirectly those public attitudes and opinions which bear on the foreign policy decisions of the Kremlin or of Peking? How do you attempt to limit the power of a totalitarian regime to engage in arbitrary or irresponsible acts which, because they endanger the peace and security of the world, are also at variance with the interests of its own peoples? I shall focus on the experience of Radio Liberty, now (1968) in its sixteenth year of broadcasting to the Soviet Union. Privately sponsored Radio Liberty is now the free world's most powerful voice directed exclusively to Soviet citizens—in Russian and sixteen other languages spoken in the U.S.S.R.

First of all, let me outline some of the obvious but extremely important problems that Radio Liberty has encountered:

(1) The Kremlin believes in maintaining its monopoly of the

information and ideas reaching all Soviet citizens—in fact, the survival of the Communist Party and preservation of the power of its
ruling elite may depend on its success in keeping this monopoly.
Radio Liberty must penetrate systematic, uninterrupted efforts to
jam all its broadcasts—not relaxed in any way when in June, 1963,
jamming of other major Western broadcasters was suspended by
the U.S.S.R.

(2) Many of the techniques and tools that are available to a radio
attempting to communicate with an open society are completely
unusable so far as the Soviet Union is concerned. If you can't take
public opinion polls or conduct audience research surveys, or, indeed, even provide for the monitoring of your radio's short wave
signal so as to determine whether it is reaching the areas and
audiences you intend to reach, you are indeed flying, if not blind,
at least in a pea-soup fog.

(3) If you cannot build a continuing dialogue with your audience, you lack one of the prime essentials of effective radio communication. The broadcaster must have an accurate image of the
listener, and of the listener's image of the broadcaster as well. Both
of these ingredients are indispensable to continuing success.

(4) Not only do you lack the tools and techniques (such as
public opinion polls and other types of sociological analysis) of
assessing from the outside what is really going on and what is the
public mood, but the ruling elite of the Soviet Union, which could
use some of these techniques for its own purposes if it wanted to,
has been both backward in applying them and even more reticent
about making available the results. Even Khrushchev, with his
hands on the levers of power, could not foresee his own ouster.

What do you do under these conditions if you are Radio Liberty? First of all, you search out former Soviet writers, scientists,
teachers, officials, and individuals from other walks of life, com-

prising more than a dozen Soviet nationalities, and equipped with a first-hand knowledge of internal conditions and a sympathetic understanding of the genuine needs and aspirations of Soviet citizens. Now living abroad, they want to help their fellow countrymen achieve a democratic society and a political system responsive and responsible to the will of the people. You do not attempt to chart any specific course of action for Soviet citizens but you ask Radio Liberty's staff to become a free voice of former citizens of the Soviet Union, representing no foreign government or foreign institution but trying to speak in the genuine interests of the Soviet citizen at home. You provide the technical facilities that will enable the émigré Russian to speak to his fellow Russian at home, the Ukrainian to his fellow Ukrainian, the Uzbek to his fellow Uzbek, with the aim of stimulating and giving cohesion to native forces in Soviet society working toward freedom from totalitarianism.

Next, you set about systematically monitoring the internal broadcasts of eighty to one hundred Soviet radio stations in Russian and other national languages so that you know *promptly* what the Soviet citizen is learning from his own media about the genuine issues that affect him. You supplement this with comprehensive and thorough review of the content of Soviet national and regional newspapers and magazines. You call on the ablest behavioral scientists you can find to tell you how to set up a continuing audience research operation that over the years will begin to build a profile of your listeners, their attitudes, their interests, their reactions to Radio Liberty's programs. In our case, we were fortunate in obtaining Dr. Max Ralis. Born in Russia, Dr. Ralis was educated in Germany, the Sorbonne, and Columbia University, where he worked under Paul Lazarsfeld. He took his Ph.D. at the University of Cologne, where his dissertation dealt with adaptation of American opinion research methods to a foreign environment. Later, he directed field research in India and Thailand for Cornell University in testing these and other Western social science techniques in underdeveloped areas.

In the early stages, your audience research division makes it possible to have long conversations or brief talks with Soviet citizens who come outside the borders of the U.S.S.R. The visitors from the outside world who go to the U.S.S.R., especially those who know one or more of the languages and have been there before, can also be questioned as to the significance of radio and television in Soviet society, listening and viewing habits, the types of program that are of greatest current interest. Thousands of such interviews have been collected and, properly coded, have been transferred to cards that can be processed by machines to show an increasingly accurate picture of the listener, and of potential listeners.

As de-Stalinization proceeds and the terror recedes a little into the background, it becomes possible to try experiments that would have seemed sheer madness at the time Radio Liberty first went on the air in 1953. Radio Liberty found by 1960 that it could engage in a dialogue with its listeners by soliciting mail. Every letter, friendly, hostile, or neutral, is acknowledged on the air, and care is taken not to identify the particular listener who writes and cause him possible unpleasantness in his home community. Radio Liberty knows that only a small fraction of the letters directed to it from its listeners succeed in reaching it through the vigilance of Soviet censors. When Radio Liberty reached the point at which the volume of letters from listeners far exceeded the quantity ever received by an outside radio from the Soviet Union, it began to experiment with honoring listener requests for nonpolitical books and articles and even phonograph records which the station offers on the air from time to time.

Radio Liberty is aided by attacks by the regime indicating clearly that those in the best position to judge know that Radio Liberty has a wide audience. Analysis of the recurring content of these attacks shows major areas of vulnerability and of audience interest.

Now what does this all add up to? In the autumn of 1962 I asked Wilbur Schramm, Director of Stanford's Institute for Communication Research, to spend a week with our audience research division in Munich and to evaluate what we were accomplishing. Dr. Schramm wrote me as follows:

> Every time I come to Munich I am impressed by the cruel conditions under which audience research has to be done here. By the rules of the game, 95 percent of all the sophisticated methods available to field researchers in western countries are foreclosed from use. I described the process of RL audience research . . . as being about like a man fishing in a murky lake without any hook on his line. He is unable to see any fish, and practically unable ever to catch a fish. Only occasionally, by being very attentive, he may feel a fish brush against his dangling line. This is the kind of job Max Ralis is trying to do. For this reason, we must be careful not to ask too much of the results of RL audience research. We have no reason to suspect that our contacts represent a probability sample. Therefore, we have no right to apply the usual statistics of reliability, and no scientific right to ask questions about the size of audience or size of segments within it. We must be very careful about saying anything about the 'profile' of the audience. . . . My impression is that your Audience Research department is doing a careful and thorough job, and exercising considerable ingenuity and imagination . . . furthermore, no recent discovery of social science, or no tool transferred from Western audience research is likely to make any magic change in the amount of information that becomes available on your audience. . . . But I feel that you can be confident that work is going forward in a solid and intelligent way, no claims are being made that should not be made, and the effort is in good hands.

We have made some progress in the years since Dr. Schramm wrote these lines to me, our data is a good deal more voluminous, and we are able to use modern data processing techniques for its analysis, but the main points he made then seem to me just as valid today.

How Does Radio Liberty Approach Its Listeners?

Now that I have set out the framework within which Radio Liberty is forced to operate, let me illustrate through a case history the approach RL makes to its listeners.

Andrei Sinyavsky and Yuli Daniel were arrested in September, 1965, but not until three months later was that fact officially acknowledged. The first mention of the arrests was made by Giancarlo Vigorelli, the Secretary-General of the Community of European Writers, at a meeting of that organization in Rome, on October 9. Vigorelli's disclosure was followed by rumors that Sinyavsky was the long-sought Abram Tertz, that Yuli Daniel was Nikolai Arzhak, and that both men would be tried according to Article 70 of the R.S.F.S.R. Criminal Code. In line with its basic principle—to inform Soviet citizens of whatever is withheld from them by their own media—RL relayed to its listeners all the unconfirmed details of the affair as they became known in the West, while carefully stressing the fact that such details *were* unconfirmed. RL set itself as its most immediate task to press for the principle Lenin enunciated in the earliest days of the Soviet Union: *glasnost*—that is, "openness," "publicity," official clarification as to whether Sinyavsky and Daniel had indeed been arrested, and for what reason. RL also avoided identifying Sinyavsky with Tertz, and Daniel with Arzhak, until, on November 11, Tertz's publisher in the West confirmed the identifications.

Not until January did the Soviet media break silence on the Sinyavsky-Daniel affair, and then it was in a Radio Moscow broadcast in English to foreign audiences!

Later in January the case officially emerged with the publication of Yeremin's article in *Izvestiya* and Zoya Kedrina's article in *Literaturnaya Gazeta*, and the Soviet press campaign to prejudge Sinyavsky was on. RL's coverage of the case during this period was concerned: 1) to advocate the principle of "presumption of innocence" against the Soviet press' practice of prejudgment; 2) to give emphasis to the view expressed abroad, especially by Western Communists, that the Sinyavsky and Daniel works were not slanderous, but expressions of legitimate criticism, which should be answered by ideas, not combated by the police and the law courts; 3) to refute the charges of "anti-Sovietism" brought against Sinyavsky and Daniel and to show listeners how Yeremin and Kedrina had unscrupulously and tendentiously manipulated out-of-context "quotations" from Tertz and Arzhak, which RL strove to do by broadcasting excerpts from and full texts of the two men's writings, without commentary; 4) to demonstrate, again through the medium of their writings, that Sinyavsky and Daniel were patriots more genuine than those who were attacking them. Some of the readings that RL broadcast at this time, notably the entire text of *The Trial Begins*, were timed to coincide with the opening of the trial in Moscow. These had been broadcast in past years from 1959 on, and RL was attacked for having done so before, during, and after the trial. Perhaps the authorities' sensitivity on this point is an indication that secretly they may share RL's view that the actual works of Tertz and Arzhak are the best proof that Sinyavsky and Daniel were not "anti-Soviet," but "anti-Stalinist."

Soviet press coverage of the trial itself made it more than clear that the trial had been prejudged. RL pointed out that the "open" trial—while an improvement, no doubt, over the summary procedures of the Stalin era—was actually not open at all, but a trial "by invitation"; even the correspondents of foreign Communist newspapers were barred. This was not surprising, considering the overwhelmingly negative foreign Communist reactions to the trial, which RL broadcast. The Soviet intelligentsia was receptive to the criticism voiced by Westerners—Communist and non-Communist alike. This seemed clear not only from the petition for clemency for Sinyavsky and Daniel that was signed by many outstanding Soviet intellectuals, and not only from the hostile questioning to which the trial judge was subjected at a meeting of the Union of Writers, but also from the fact that "off-the-record" comments made by Soviet intellectuals and students appeared to reflect the main lines of this criticism; namely, that the trial had been immensely damaging to the Soviet "public image"; that it was doubtful which was the more effective anti-Soviet propaganda, the writings of Tertz and Arzhak or the trial of Tertz and Arzhak; that Soviet justice, rather than two writers, had been on trial; and that Soviet citizens themselves really could not conclude anything about the "anti-Soviet" content of the two men's writings, since their actual works had not been made available to the public.

The trial was officially over in February 1966, but in actuality it continued. Numerous documents reached the West, including an almost complete stenographic report of the trial, protests by prominent Soviet writers and by the wives of the accused, and a letter from Daniel—never published—to the newspaper *Izvestiya*. RL has reacted promptly to these with full broadcast treatment, in order to keep listeners fully informed of domestic as well as foreign reaction against the verdict and sentence. Predictably, this has brought accusations from the authorities that RL is using the Sinyavsky-Daniel affair for the purposes of "anti-Soviet propaganda."

In its issue of April 1966, *Encounter* printed a very interesting report by British United Press describing dialogues between Soviet citizens and a Communist Party spokesman in the crowd outside the courtroom. The discussion seemed to have the most remarkable similarity to the kind of dialogue that Radio Liberty had been holding. For example, a youth said, "They could very well have held a trial in a larger hall. We ought to be allowed inside." The Communist in the crowd replied, "We have our representatives; the Communist Party members are inside." And the crowd booed. Then somebody said, "Well, look, it's all reported in the papers." And a man said, "*You* can believe that. We can't trust it." A girl spoke up, "No one knows what's going on in there. Why must we listen to the British Broadcasting Corporation to hear the facts about it?" And the Communist said, "The foreign press is distorting the facts." Someone replied, "How do you know, have you read the foreign press?" And the Communist, hard-pressed, answered, "No, but I know." Another question, "Why don't they publish the books here so we can draw our own conclusions? This is something for public opinion. The public must judge." And the conversation continued in this fashion.

I wrote earlier that in its pretrial coverage RL stressed the principle of "presumption of innocence" against prejudgment by the press. It may be mere coincidence that after the trial this same line was echoed by an outspoken legal commentator in an official Soviet publication. In any case, it was not the first time that a reform proposal originally put forth by Radio Liberty has found public expression and even, in some cases, adoption within the Soviet Union.

Is Radio Liberty Making Any Headway in Its Broadcasts?

Mindful of Dr. Schramm's strictures, I shall not attempt to claim that Radio Liberty can be shown to be directly affecting those public attitudes and opinions which bear on the Soviet government's foreign policy decisions. Indeed, I say that Radio Liberty may continue its broadcasts for a generation and never be able to *prove* such an influence. But there is encouraging evidence for those of us who believe that something like a public mood is developing inside the Soviet Union, which the present rulers (or their successors) cannot disregard.

One of the most important studies of communication inside the closed society is being carried out at the Massachusetts Institute of Technology by Dr. Ithiel de Sola Pool. He made public for the first time some of his preliminary findings at a conference Radio Liberty sponsored jointly with New York University in November 1965. Here is what he said about communicating with the peoples of the U.S.S.R.:

> Most of those things of a positive character that are happening in the Soviet Union today are explainable only in terms of the influence of the West, for which the most important single channel is radio. . . . There is now enough communication to keep us part of a single civilization, to keep us influencing each other, to assure that any Western idea circulates in the Soviet Union too. The pessimistic expectation that totalitarianism could develop an accepted heinous civilization of its own by 1984 or any other year has been defeated primarily by the forces of communication and above all, by international radio.

The important Soviet ideological journal *Kommunist*, after mentioning Radio Liberty by name, put it this way:

> In our time, when there is a radio in almost every home, to fail to mention any event . . . is to give freedom of action to the falsifications of bourgeois propagandists. . . . We cannot fail to admit that the bourgeois information agencies have attained a high degree of efficiency, responding immediately, as they do, to everything that happens in the world, while we are sometimes late. . . . The first announcement sometimes makes a greater impression.

This was put in another way in a *New York Times* report quoting Soviet poet Yevgeny Yevtushenko on experiences during his fall from political grace:

You know I got hundreds of letters from ordinary people all over Russia who had read my poems. They sent money, more than $1,000. I sent it all back, all except 3 rubles from a little girl. I sent her a poem instead because she said she wanted to be a poet. The point is that the people didn't let me down—and public opinion means something in Russia today. The new Soviet leadership respects this. They are practical men; they listen to the people's wants.

Letters reaching Radio Liberty from its listeners confirm the emergence of independent thinking.

Your radio station, as it were, removed from before my eyes the curtain of mist created by our press.

What do I like in your broadcasts? . . . those news items and questions which I am unable to learn from our Soviet broadcasts, books, and newspapers.

I listen to your broadcasts and I feel that you stand for the truth.

You tell me such interesting things. They open up a new world for me, new horizons.

Radio Liberty's influence, according to its listeners, is based on its ability to present the facts and events in a truthful and forthright way, its competence in Soviet affairs, its knowledge of the psychological climate of the country and of the mentality of its listeners, as well as the economic conditions prevailing in the Soviet Union.

The listeners we know about are young (two-thirds under thirty). They are deeply concerned about prospects for peace and war, disillusioned with ideology, passionately curious about the outside world and eager to identify with it, and inclined to be impatient to enjoy the fruits of past sacrifice. While proud of Soviet space and technological achievements, they sense keenly the discrepancy between these and their mediocre standard of living.

I believe that effective communication with a closed society is possible and can be of great importance in affecting that society's domestic and foreign policy decisions. I believe, too, that effectiveness can be increased by research in which social scientists and practitioners collaborate. I would like to suggest a few research avenues which might be investigated.

Areas of Social Science Research of Interest to Public Diplomacy

Although I am myself most intimately concerned with radio, and presume I must be bracketed with the "literate people" who Marshall McLuhan says are unable "to grasp the language and message . . . [of] the tribal drum of radio," I am not sure that this "hot" medium *is* the message—at least not when heard through jamming. We need *agents provocateurs des idées* like Mr. McLuhan—and we need some solid work in a number of areas of the social sciences:

1. THE SENSE OF HEARING

a. *Do all people hear alike?* Let me start with an analogy from the biological sciences. As early as 1932 the late Dr. Albert F. Blakeslee of the Carnegie Institute of Genetics was demonstrating the remarkable behavioral differences people display in their reactions to the same stimuli—in these cases differences in taste and smell. Subjects' taste thresholds differed and also the kind of sensation which they appeared to get from the same substance varied. For example, at an exhibit at the American Museum of Natural History in 1932, over 6,000 people tasted slips of paper treated with an alcoholic solution of PTC (phenyl-thio-carbamide). Twenty per cent couldn't taste this at all, and among those who could taste it, although a majority found it was bitter, there were still 5 per cent who found it salty, 2 per cent who found it sweet, and another 5 per cent who found it sour. Dr. Blakeslee showed that differences in ability to taste PTC were innate and hereditary and concluded that "there is no reason to believe that differences in ability to taste other substances are not also innate and hereditary."

Some of the most authoritative of modern researchers, however, believe that taste and smell preferences are composed largely of socially determined attitudes plus a few innate responses. Our noses seem to start out with very few likes or dislikes and almost all of our attitudes about smells are determined by cultural pressures and personal experiences.

My layman's conclusion from what the biological scientists and the geneticists have been experimenting with in differences in taste and smell was that no two people are exactly alike in the sensory reactions and probably never have been. I have often wondered what the implications might be for those of us who are trying to communicate primarily through the sense of hearing, by radio.

b. *Hearing and perception.* We in radio need to know far more than we do about perception of the world through the sense of hearing. The work already done on the sense of vision, if systematically applied to the sense of hearing, has implications that should be of enormous significance for all of us who must communicate by radio.

2. REALITY WORLDS IN CLOSED SOCIETIES

a. *Cantril's work.* We are indebted to postwar work by social scientists, who have given us a greater understanding of the nature of our reality worlds. Dr. Handley Cantril, Adelbert Ames, and some of their colleagues in the field of transactional psychology have taught us a great deal about human perception. Dr. Cantril and others tell us that "a person's reality world can only be altered through experience, not through indoctrination and dictum alone."[2] Actually, Dr. Cantril wrote this particular sentence after a visit to the Soviet Union in November 1958. He also concluded that the experience of Soviet citizens "has not yet been sufficient to give them a clear idea of what they do want."

The communicator to the closed society must meditate prayerfully over this psychologist's conclusion that

we revise our assumptions infrequently, if at all, solely because of any factual knowledge or information we acquire but do not test out in our own experience or the experience we may share with other people. It definitely appears as though we must experience the consequences of action or shared action if there is to be any impact on our reality worlds.[3]

b. *Self-portraits of closed societies.* An important dimension is being added to our knowledge of reality worlds by systematic psychological studies surveying representative samples of the adult populations in many nations. Development of the self-anchoring striving scale helps to focus in peoples' own terms what they are actually feeling, and what their assumptions are. What are their hopes and their fears? What are the effects of circumstances on the outlooks which people hold for themselves and their nations? Although such a study has not yet been made for the Soviet Union, such surveys were made in Yugoslavia in the spring of 1962 and at the same time in Poland.

3. COMMUNICATIONS FLOW IN CLOSED SOCIETIES

Of very great practical importance should be the results of the study being conducted under the direction of Ithiel Pool, to which I have already referred, on the communication system itself within a closed society, such as that of the U.S.S.R.

4. RADIO AND CLOSED SOCIETIES: LISTENERS AND NONLISTENERS

In another area I would like to see the gap between the researcher and theoretician and the operator and communicator greatly reduced. In a closed society, do people who listen to Western broad-casts form attitudes more favorable to our Western policies and points of view? In effect, I am asking that we hold all the variables that we can constant and see whether there is a difference between listeners to Western broadcasts and those who do not listen. What we are looking for is the answer to such questions as these: Does the act of listening produce different attitudes in listeners from those of nonlisteners? Do people actually behave differently be-cause they have listened to foreign broadcasts? If this is the case, is it possible to predict in what ways they will act differently?

The experience of Radio Liberty, ranging over a period which has seen the transition from the intense Cold War of Stalin's last days to growing hopes for lasting relaxation of Soviet-American tensions, has shown that as access to a closed society improves there is a corresponding increase in the role of foreign broadcast-ing. This in turn places heavier demands on the competence, creativity, and—above all—integrity of those who originate the broadcasts.

As satellites and other technological advances present radical new opportunities for international cross-cultural communication, perhaps ultimately by point-to-point television transmission, the challenge to the communicators is far greater than ever before. The techniques of advertising or of wartime psychological warfare, aimed at inducing enemy soldiers to surrender or defect, have little relevance here, where the objective is to promote stable relation-ships between peoples of different countries. We look to the social sciences to help us find needed new directions in our work.

12

THE CONVERGENCE
OF SOCIAL SYSTEMS

John Scott
Time Magazine

While visiting the Soviet Union in the fall of 1965, I partici-
pated in a presentation to a group of Ministry of Foreign Trade
officials. The idea for such an event had germinated when my colleagues and I learned a year before that the Soviet government had
organized an advertising agency. We approached the Soviet Embassy with the proposition that we offer a program, in the style
and tradition of U.S. advertising agencies, before the newly formed
Soviet agency and Russian businessmen, manufacturers, and foreign trade officials. As we had anticipated, their reply was a laconic,
"We'll relay this information and let you know." About six weeks
thereafter we were notified that the answer was "yes."

After preparing nearly 100 colored slides showing pictorial graphs captioned in Russian and booklets used in the United States (translated into Russian) on the subject of merchandising and advertising, my colleagues and I journeyed to Moscow. During a preliminary lunch with Mr. Vassiliev, president of the Soviet Union's new ad agency, he explained his interest in the matter: "I'm very happy you gentlemen are here. You're going to help me do my job."

We asked that he explain further. "You see," he answered, "I've been appointed by the Party to try to introduce modern merchandising and advertising techniques into those parts of the Soviet economy where they might be useful. We manufacture items that we think could and should be exported to the dollar-sterling area— automotive products, aircraft, watches, electronic equipment, etc. My job is to persuade those in control to adopt some of these modern techniques. And frequently they are very uncooperative. Recently the president of our watch manufacturing trust told me, 'Look, I make watches and they work, so why should I advertise?' Now you gentlemen are going to help me persuade them."

Invitations were issued in our names through the ad agency to seventy-five persons whom Mr. Vassiliev selected—high officials in trusts and manufacturing—for 3:30 P.M. at the National Hotel. The U.S. Embassy warned us that a 50 per cent draw on invitations for any sort of function for Soviet citizens was considered good and that we should not be surprised if people arrived late or many didn't appear at all. It was both unexpected and gratifying, therefore, when at 3:35 P.M. there were seventy-five people in the room.

I made the presentation in Russian, followed by forty minutes of questions from the audience: "How much does it cost to put a particular advertisement in a particular edition, and what have been the sales curves achieved by organizations which have done so in the past?" One question made us smile. A gentleman asked, "How many advertisements do we have to buy to determine the editorial policy of *Time* magazine?" We answered that it wasn't for sale. I later learned that the person asking the question had lived briefly in the Middle East. In this context the question was not as unreasonable as it might have sounded, for in some areas of that region there are newspapers of which every column is on sale by the inch.

After the questions began to flag, we moved into another room where tables were groaning with food. The last guest departed at about 10:30 P.M. During the whole performance no one mentioned Vietnam, American imperialism, or the class struggle. The conversation mainly concerned techniques of production and sales of certain categories of commodities in competitive overseas markets.

The experience was interesting and particularly rewarding for me because I later had the opportunity to talk at greater length to many of the gentlemen whom I had met that day. But the experience was even more significant as an expression of a movement toward reform in business management and economic policy in the U.S.S.R. Kosygin's speech at the September 1965 plenum of the central committee of the Communist Party enlarged upon more theoretical suggestions made earlier by persons such as Professor Evsei Leberman about streamlining the Soviet business administration.

Because of the lack of interest in the Soviet Union in the mechanisms of distribution, huge inventories of unsold consumer goods had accumulated on stores' shelves and large inventories of unneeded materials—steel, glass, cement, and equipment—had accumulated in the back yards of Soviet industrial enterprises. There being no charge on either working or fixed capital, such surpluses did not cost anything. The business manager frequently reasoned, "Well, if I don't need steel this week, I might need some next week, and if I don't need steel, perhaps I can trade it for glass or something I do need."

In order to eliminate all this highly wasteful and expensive operation, Kosygin suggested the introduction of a flat 5 per cent fixed interest charge on both fixed and working capital in the Soviet Union. He further suggested a vast increase in the individual authority and initiative of the business manager, who until recently had been assigned by the Central Planning Authority in Moscow. The organizational structure of most industries had resembled that of a military unit, specifying a certain number of persons in each rank in an inflexible structure and a predetermined, inflexible wage scale for each level. Kosygin's suggestion gave the business manager the authority to eliminate redundant positions and unnecessary departments, to create needed new departments, and to fire inefficient or unneeded individuals. He could also bargain with the trade unions about wages, give engineers and executives incentive bonuses, and regulate their wage scales. The business manager was also to be able to negotiate with the outlet through which his commodities would be sold and with sources supplying raw materials.

The position of the Soviet business manager would thus approach that of the manager of a large factory owned by a major company in the United States. He would be a salaried executive and his reputation and his bonus would be based largely on the profitability of his enterprise. He would be well paid but could be peremptorily fired should he fail to produce or to function well with top management. He would depend on top management for large amounts of investment capital and for major decisions such as plant relocation or alteration of product line. But smaller decisions would be in his hands: the development of new products, merchandising markets, and production techniques. Between Soviet and U.S. business managers there would be obvious differences in nomenclature and circumstances. The regional manager of General Motors would almost certainly own some General Motors stock, whereas the Soviet executive would be able to salt away earnings from a State savings bank at 4 per cent interest, but would not be able to acquire any equity.

Other changes embodied in the Kosygin reforms would effect basic changes in the operation of the Soviet economy. However, to say that such changes would constitute the introduction of capitalism into the Soviet economy would be erroneous. The essence of capitalism is the private ownership and operation of the means of production, and the essence of socialism is the public ownership and operation of these means. There has been no indication of taking the means of production away from the state in the U.S.S.R. On the other hand, a number of techniques representing important aspects of the free enterprise or modified free enterprise economy are being adopted by Soviet leadership.

This complex of reform moves would have been more appropriate in the Soviet Union in the mid-1930's than in the mid-1960's. By the mid-30's the number of commodities in the Soviet economy had proliferated to a point where Central Planning could no longer efficiently trace the economic trajectory of each pair of shoes and small commodity through the production cycle. During these years, many changes were being made in the economics of the Western world; Adam Smith and Ricardo no longer ruled. The Soviet economists, however, were unable to tinker with their economic system because of domination by Joseph Stalin. The system was so rigorous that deviation was punished by drastic surgery which discouraged others from expression of new ideas.

Consequently, the Soviet Union witnessed a generation-long delay in setting up reforms which I believe constitute their side of a process of convergence. It has left them with a residual hangover of preconvergence or prereform phraseology which permeates the daily press. The daily press is one of the most retrogressive and reactionary aspects of Soviet life, introducing a great degree of ambivalence into both domestic and foreign policy.

Conversations I had with Soviet citizens concerning the Vietnamese conflict illustrate this point. The government of the U.S.-S.R. has frequently expressed its opinions on Vietnam; it condemns the actions of the United States, believing them to be aggressive. The Soviet Union has contributed economic and military aid to North Vietnam while carefully avoiding association with the Viet Cong; they have preferred to deal with Hanoi, rather than with the liberation front or its army. When questioned about their feelings concerning Vietnam, most Soviet citizens usually begin by repeating without much enthusiasm the official Soviet position with whatever degree of sophistication their educational levels warrant. Afterward, however, they usually add, "You know, to be frank, we understand that your presence in South Vietnam is not only useful to the United States, but it's also important to the Soviet Union. If you left there, the Chinese would take that whole area within the next few years, and we'd have real trouble with them. But we can't say this publicly."

In one case I took this dialogue a step further—with the editor of a Soviet magazine who I knew would give a frank opinion. I told him that many of my colleagues in Washington believed that a substantial group in the Pentagon had considered making a pre-emptive strike against the nuclear potential of Communist China, but had been vetoed by the President. I asked him what the Russian reaction would have been had this step been taken or what it would be if the step were taken in the future.

He answered thoughtfully, "We Russians may find it necessary at some point in the future to undertake a pre-emptive strike against the nuclear potential of West Germany. If we do this, however, I am sure that (a) we will let you know beforehand, and

(b) we will so contrive this pre-emptive strike that it will be a response to a provocation by the West Germans, in order to avoid activating the automatic clauses in the NATO alliance. If you find it necessary to undertake a strike against Communist China, we hope that you will be similarly considerate of our feelings."

This fairly sophisticated attitude bespoke the ambivalence of opinion in the Soviet Union, which has grown largely from the conflict between substantial convergence in the economy and un-reconstructed phraseology—the semantics of the public press and the institutional superstructure of foreign policy.

The United States has been under far less pressure from narrow sectarians to maintain an orthodoxy in economic theory, and within my lifetime there have been many very substantial changes. Within the last generation a series of so-called "control" organizations such as the Securities Exchange Commission, the Interstate Commerce Commission, and the Federal Communications Commission have been created, charged with the imposition of certain restraints on private enterprise in the areas of communication and commerce. These restraints usually involve such things as prices that may be charged for services and the circumstances under which services may be abolished. On the local level, the institution of zoning has imposed severe restrictions on the type of building one can erect on a piece of land he owns, where it can be situated, and how many people or how many families may occupy it. A series of rather special organizations like the Railroad Commission of the State of Texas have appeared. This body acts like a national planning institution in determining and enforcing the quantity of petroleum that private petroleum companies can produce annually in the United States. Also, we have evolved an agricultural system under which six to eight billion dollars a year are spent on regulating the production of crops. A large part of the money pays farm-ers *not* to produce basic agricultural commodities which have firmly pegged prices. This agreement cannot be violated by the farmer without severe penalties.

All of these developments in the United States represent an adaptation of our economic theory and practice to modern technology. They represent the adjustment of the U.S. economy to the classical contradiction of capitalism, as described by Marx—the contradiction between social production and private expropriation. They represent a degree of convergence on our side. Like the Russians, however, we have left much of our terminology and phraseology unrevised. We still use words like capitalism, democracy, and freedom in inaccurate contexts which introduce a degree of ambivalence into the formulation of foreign policy.

As an example, I shall cite the reporting of important international events—by the Chinese and by the United States. In discussing international events, the Chinese use phraseology that sounds strange if one is unaccustomed to reading publications from Communist China. For example, in reporting on trade talks which culminated in several agreements between the Soviet Union and Japan, *The Peking Review* said: "An important step in the U.S.-Soviet collaboration for world domination is the Soviet Union's stepping up of collusion with the Japanese reactionaries." On the tricontinental congress of Communist functionaries which took place in Havana, the same publication wrote:

The two-faced tactics of the Khrushchev revisionists were especially vicious on the question of Vietnam. The Soviet delegate pretended to support the Vietnamese people in their struggle against U.S. aggression, but he did not dare to condemn the U.S. in strong terms. When the Johnson administration was launching its peace offensive, the Soviet delegate advocated "the realization of peace in Vietnam." This was obviously acting in coordination with U.S. imperialism. What Khrushchev revisionists are advocating is certainly not anti-imperialism, since they regard the common enemy of the peoples of Asia, Africa, and Latin America as the one with whom they should collaborate. They are bent on taking united action with the U.S. imperialists in pursuit of the domination of the world.

An interesting comparison is the Washington version of the same Havana conference.

Soviet chief delegate Shary Rhedtoff made what amounted to a guerrilla declaration of war against specific Latin American countries. He pledged Soviet support, money and weapons for national liberation movements in four specific countries and invited guerrillas to rise elsewhere in the hemisphere with the assurance of Soviet support. Military sources who contributed to the U.S. evaluation of the Havana Communist conference feel that the subversion, sabotage, terror and general guerrilla tactics advocated there will shortly be broadened and intensified over all of Latin America in response to the Soviet Communist efforts to harass the United States in this hemisphere.

These discrepancies in the reporting of one conference exemplify the basis upon which foreign policy, both in the area of public diplomacy and strict foreign office terms, is formulated. And the obvious result of this kind of ambivalence and failure of both sides to keep the phraseology and thinking up to date is confusion and unnecessary conflict. If the United States talked about order and development instead of democracy and freedom, we might be better understood. The concept of freedom is to a degree a contradiction to the concept of control and order. When we constantly talk about the defense of freedom in certain areas, we confuse ourselves and others.

In the Soviet Union there are red and white signs on numerous buildings which read, "Forward to Communism Throughout the World." I asked some citizens precisely what was meant by these words. Responses varied; a graduate student replied, "Well, this is not referring to the current context of things, for although we know that theoretically capitalism is moribund and dying, it's obvious to all of us that it still does everything better than we do."

The Soviet citizen's formulation of what communism and the class-less society throughout the world might mean is comparable to the fuzzy ideological terms in which a U.S. citizen might define the brotherhood of man.

I suggest that a process is occurring which in Aristotelian language may be called the evolution of a golden mean. In the language of Communism it is called dialectical materialism—a process through which a thesis and an antithesis reach a synthesis. I am not suggesting that this convergence is by any means complete in U.S.-Soviet relations. There remain vast areas of difference in concrete economic terms. We operate different kinds of systems. But a degree of convergence is being achieved, and thus far, leadership in both societies has exaggerated the differences and underplayed the increasing similarities, confusing the formulation of foreign policy on both sides.

It is my belief that a thorough study of the chemistry of convergence and the elimination of fuzzy thinking and obsolete terminology in the formulation of public and foreign diplomacy would constitute a major step forward for both sides and would increase the possibility of living through this century without a major military conflict.

NOTES

3. Wedge: Communication Analysis and Comprehensive Diplomacy

1. Hadley Cantril, *The Pattern of Human Concerns* (New Brunswick, N.J.: Rutgers University Press, 1965).

2. Harold Nicolson, *The Evolution of Diplomacy* (New York: Collier Books, 1962; first published 1954).

3. William Hayter, *The Diplomacy of the Great Powers* (New York: Macmillan, 1961).

4. Lloyd A. Free, below, p. 48.

5. Harold Sprout and Margaret Sprout, *Foundations of International Politics* (Princeton, N.J.: D. Van Nostrand, 1962).

6. Robert Rossow, "The Professionalization of the New Diplomacy," *World Politics*, XIV (July 1962), pp. 561-575.

7. W. Phillips Davison, *International Political Communication* (New York: Praeger, 1965).

8. Walter Lippmann, quoted in Wright Miller's *Russians as People* (New York: Dutton, 1961).

9. Controversies which have arisen in the United States since this study only serve to strengthen the point, for most of the arguments have turned on the adequacy of the evidence and the Warren Commission's procedures, not on a conspiratorial theory as the starting point. Even those polemicists who obviously favor such a view are careful to search for evidential or procedural flaws to support their case. A public opinion survey by the Gallup poll showed that 71 per cent of a national sample in 1963 had doubts that Lee Harvey Oswald acted alone. In 1966, 64 per cent were still in doubt. The American people are still weighing the evidence.

10. Bryant Wedge and Cyril Muromcew, "Psychological Factors in Soviet Disarmament Negotiation," *Journal of Conflict Resolution*, 9 (March 1965), pp. 18-36.

11. Ralph K. White, " 'Socialism' and 'Capitalism'," *Foreign Affairs*, 44 (January, 1966), pp. 216-228.

12. Bryant Wedge, *Visitors to the United States and How They See Us* (Princeton, N.J.: D. Van Nostrand, 1965).

13. Bryant Wedge, *The Political Utility of Multilateral Force* (Princeton, N.J.: Institute for the Study of National Behavior, September, 1964).

14. Edmund Glenn, "A Cognitive Approach to the Analysis of Culture and Cultural Evolution," *General Systems Yearbook*, vol. XI, ed. Ludwig von Bertalanffy and Anatol Rapoport (Ann Arbor, Mich., 1966), pp. 115-132.

15. Robert Rossow's otherwise excellent paper (see note 5) fails to draw this essential distinction and consequently sets virtually impossible tasks in diplomatic training and functioning.

4. Free: Public Opinion Research

1. For books on the general subject of public opinion, see particularly *The American People and Foreign Policy* by Gabriel A. Almond

(New York: Praeger, 1962); *Public Opinion and American Democracy* by the late V. O. Key, Jr. (New York: Knopf, 1964); and several related books by Alfred Hero.

2. For a historical account of U.S. efforts to influence foreign opinion, see Howland Sargeant's chapter on "American Information and Cultural Representation Overseas" in *The Representation of the United States Abroad,* edited by Vincent M. Barnett, Jr. (New York: Praeger, 1965). For a broader treatment of international communications in general, see *International Political Communication* by W. Phillips Davison, published for the Council on Foreign Relations (New York: Praeger, 1965).

3. "Trends of Opinion during World War II: Some Guides to Interpretation," *Public Opinion Quarterly,* Spring 1948.

4. Published by the Institute for International Social Research, Princeton, N.J., 1960.

5. *Attitudes of the Cuban People toward the Castro Regime,* by Lloyd A. Free, published as a monograph by the Institute for International Social Research, Princeton, N.J.

6. "The American Image Will Take Care of Itself," *New York Times Magazine,* February 28, 1965.

7. *Some International Implications of the Political Psychology of Brazilians,* by Lloyd A. Free, published in monograph form by the Institute for International Social Research, Princeton, N.J., 1961.

8. Lloyd A. Free and Hadley Cantril, *The Political Beliefs of Americans* (New Brunswick, N.J.: Rutgers University Press, 1968).

9. Spring 1963.

10. For one study of an American elite, see *American Business and Public Policy* by Raymond A. Bauer, Ithiel de Sola Pool, and Lewis Anthony Dexter (New York: Atherton Press, 1963), which undoubtedly was taken into account by U.S. policy-makers in handling the Kennedy trade bill. Also Bernard C. Cohen's booklet on *The Influence of Non-Government Groups on Foreign Policy Making* (World Peace Foundation, 1959). One of the largest studies on elite opinion abroad is still being conducted by Daniel Lerner in western Europe, having to do with attitudes of the elite toward European integration (see Daniel Lerner, "Interviewing European Elites," *Polls* magazine, Fall 1966). When it comes to governmental elites, our own Institute for International Social Research has questioned cross-sections of national

legislators in ten countries to date, the first series of which were recounted in *Six Allies and a Neutral* by Lloyd A. Free (Glencoe, Ill.: Free Press, 1959). Subsequent studies have been reported on in various of our monographs.

11. *Some Indications of World-Wide Public Opinion toward the U.S. and the U.S.S.R.*, Research and Reference Service, USIA, July 1963.

12. USIA has done much research on different aspects of the image of America abroad; a good deal of these data have by now been declassified. Dr. h. c. K. G. von Stackelberg reports that his Emhid-Institute in West Germany has done surveys about the German image in France, England, five Southeast Asian countries, and six Latin American nations for the use of the German press and information agency. See also "The Image of America Abroad" (a symposium under the chairmanship of Leo P. Crespi), *Public Opinion Quarterly*, Fall 1960; Ithiel de Sola Pool and Kali Prasad, "Indian Student Images of Foreign Peoples," *Public Opinion Quarterly*, Fall, 1958; Franz M. Joseph (ed.), *As Others See Us: The United States through Foreign Eyes* (Princeton University Press, 1959); and William Buchanan and Hadley Cantril, *How Nations See Each Other* (Urbana, Ill.: University of Illinois Press, 1953).

13. My study, *The Political Beliefs of Americans*, cited above, shows that seven out of ten Americans agree that the United States should cooperate fully with the United Nations. Dr. Henry Durant, of the British Gallup Poll, reports similar support in the United Kingdom, which goes so far that 60 per cent would favor a United Nations police force, even if relatives of theirs had to serve in it.

14. Working through local outfits, our Institute for International Social Research, for example, has been able to conduct surveys in some twenty-one countries in all parts of the world, including, incidentally, two Communist nations, Yugoslavia and Poland. Most of the results are analyzed in Hadley Cantril's *The Pattern of Human Concerns* (New Brunswick, N.J.: Rutgers University Press, 1965).

15. See the chapter entitled "The Study of Modal Personality and Socio-cultural Systems," by Alex Inkeles and Daniel J. Levinson, in the *Handbook of Social Psychology* (Cambridge, Mass.: Addison-Wesley, 1954); and *Political Culture and Political Development* by Lucian W. Pye and Sidney Verba (Princeton University Press, 1965).

6. Mead: The Importance of National Cultures

1. Margaret Mead and Rhoda Metraux, eds., *The Study of Culture at a Distance* (Chicago: University of Chicago Press, 1953); Margaret Mead and Rhoda Metraux, "The Anthropology of Human Conflict," in *The Nature of Human Conflict*, ed. Elton B. McNeil (Englewood Cliffs, N.J.: Prentice-Hall, 1965), pp. 116-138.

2. Geoffrey Gorer, "Themes in Japanese Culture," in *Transactions of The New York Academy of Sciences*, Ser. 2, 1943, 5: 106-124.

3. Robert S. Lynd and Helen M. Lynd, *Middletown* (New York: Harcourt, Brace, 1929); Robert S. Lynd and Helen M. Lynd, *Middletown in Transition* (New York: Harcourt, Brace, 1937).

4. W. Lloyd Warner and Paul S. Lunt, *The Social Life of a Modern Community*, Yankee City Series, vol. 1 (New Haven: Yale University Press, 1941); W. Lloyd Warner and Paul S. Lunt, *The Status System of a Modern Community*, Yankee City Series, vol. 2 (New Haven: Yale University Press, 1942); W. Lloyd Warner and Leo Srole, *The Social Systems of American Ethnic Groups*, Yankee City Series, vol. 3 (New Haven: Yale University Press, 1945); W. Lloyd Warner and J. O. Low, *The Social System of the Modern Factory*, Yankee City Series, vol. 4 (New Haven: Yale University Press, 1947); W. Lloyd Warner, *Yankee City*, abridged ed. (New Haven: Yale University Press, 1963).

5. Margaret Mead, "The Study of National Character," in *The Policy Sciences*, Daniel Lerner and Harold D. Lasswell, eds. (Stanford: Stanford University Press, 1951), pp. 70-84.

6. Mead and Metraux, *The Study of Culture at a Distance*.

7. Gregory Bateson, "An Analysis of the Nazi Film *Hitlerjunge Quex*," in Mead and Metraux, *The Study of Culture at a Distance*, pp. 302-314.

8. Gregory Bateson, "Morale and National Character," in *Civilian Morale*, Goodwin Watson, ed. (Boston: Houghton, Mifflin, 1942), pp. 71-91.

9. Ruth Benedict, *Thai Culture and Behavior*, war-time study dated September, 1943 (Ithaca, N.Y.: Cornell University, Southeast Asia Program, Data Papers, No. 4, 1954; mimeographed).

10. Margaret Mead, "The Application of Anthropological Tech-

niques to Cross-National Communication," in *Transactions of The New York Academy of Sciences*, Ser. 2, 1947, 9: 133-152; Margaret Mead, "A Case History in Cross-National Communications," in *The Communication of Ideas*, Lyman Bryson, ed. (New York: Institute for Religion and Social Studies, 1948), pp. 209-229.

11. Geoffrey Gorer, *Exploring English Character* (New York: Criterion Books, 1955).

12. Ruth Benedict, *The Chrysanthemum and the Sword* (Boston: Houghton Mifflin, 1946).

13. Rhoda Metraux and Margaret Mead, *Themes in French Culture: A Preface to a Study of French Community*, Hoover Institute Studies, Ser. D, Communities, No. 1 (Stanford: Stanford University Press, 1954); Laurence Wylie, *Village in the Vaucluse* (Cambridge: Harvard University Press, 1957); Laurence Wylie, ed., *Chanzeaux: A Village in Anjou* (Cambridge: Harvard University Press, 1966).

14. Geoffrey Gorer and John Rickman, *The People of Great Russia* (London: Cresset Press, 1949); Margaret Mead, *Soviet Attitudes Toward Authority* (New York: McGraw-Hill, 1951).

15. Margaret Mead, ed., *Cultural Patterns and Technical Change: A Manual Prepared by the World Federation for Mental Health*, Tensions and Technology Series (Paris: Unesco, 1953); Conrad M. Arensberg and Arthur N. Niehoff, *Introducing Social Change: A Manual for Americans Overseas* (Chicago: Aldine, 1964); Charles Erasmus, *Man Takes Control* (Indianapolis: Bobbs-Merrill, 1965).

16. Margaret Mead, "The Rights of Primitive Peoples," *Foreign Affairs* (1967), 45: 304-318.

17. John Walsh, "Social Sciences: Cancellation of Camelot after Row in Chile Brings Research under Scrutiny," *Science* (1965), 149, 3689: 1209-1211.

18. Raymond Dennett and Joseph E. Johnson, eds., *Negotiating with the Russians* (Boston: World Peace Foundation, 1951).

19. Geoffrey Gorer, *The American People* (New York: Norton, 1948, rev. ed. 1964); Margaret Mead, *And Keep Your Powder Dry* (New York: Morrow, 1942, rev. ed. 1965); Jules Henry, *Culture against Man* (New York: Random House, 1963); Solon T. Kimball and Marion Pearsall, *Talladega Story* (University, Ala.: University of Alabama Press, 1954; Oscar Lewis, "The Culture of Poverty," *Scientific American* (1966) 215, 4: 19-25.

20. Alvin Wolfe, "The African Mineral Industry: Evolution of a Supranational Level of Integration," *Social Problems* (1963) 11: 153-164.

7. Coser: The Role of Groups: Contributions of Sociology

1. John Dewey, *The Public and Its Problems* (New York: Henry Holt, 1927), p. 188.

2. James Bryce, *The American Commonwealth*, Vol. II (New York: Macmillan, 1900), p. 250.

3. David Truman, *The Governmental Process* (New York: Knopf, 1960), p. 19.

4. Cf. Gabriel Almond, *The American People and Foreign Policy* (New York: Harcourt, Brace, 1950).

5. Cf. H. Eckstein, ed., *Internal War* (New York: The Free Press, 1964), p. 22 and passim.

6. Alexis de Tocqueville, *Democracy in America*, ed. Phillips Bradley, Vol. II (New York: Knopf, 1953), p. 111.

7. Cf. Truman, p. 518 and passim.

8. Hans Morgenthau, *Politics Among Nations*, 2nd ed. (New York: Knopf, 1954), p. 510.

9. Thomas Hobbes, *Behemoth*, from *Works*, ed. Sir William Molesworth (London: J. Bohn, 1839-45), vol. VI, p. 259.

9. Maynard: The Language of International Communication

1. Evelyn Waugh, *A Little Learning: An Autobiography—The Early Years* (Boston: Little, Brown, 1964), p. 139.

2. Alfred Korzybski, *Science and Sanity*, 2nd edition (Lancaster, Pa.: Science Press, 1941) p. 90.

3. Aldous Huxley, "A Philosopher's Visionary Prediction," *Playboy* magazine, November 1963.

4. "Innovator—Enrico Fermi: Open Door to Atomic Age," *Newsfront*, April 1964.

5. C. E. Silberman, "Is Technology Taking Over?" *Fortune* magazine, February 1966.

11. Communications to Open and Closed Societies

1. *Report of the Twenty-fifth American Assembly: The United States and Canada*, p. 7.
2. Hadley Cantril, *Soviet Leaders and Mastery Over Man* (New Brunswick, N.J.: Rutgers University Press, 1960), p. 110.
3. Hadley Cantril, *The Politics of Despair* (New York: Basic Books, 1958), p. 26.